crushed

~~the~~ the ~~boys~~ life that never liked me back

a memoir-ish

kiersten lyons

A REGALO PRESS BOOK
ISBN: 979-8-88845-838-9
ISBN (eBook): 979-8-88845-839-6

crushed:
the boys that never liked me back
© 2025 by Kiersten Lyons
All Rights Reserved

Cover Design by Jim Villaflores
Interior Typesetting, Composition, and Doodles by Alana Mills

Publishing Team:
Founder and Publisher – Gretchen Young
Managing Editor – Madeline Sturgeon
Production Manager – Kate Harris
Production Editor – Rachel Paul

As part of the mission of Regalo Press, a donation is being made to Big Brothers Big Sisters as chosen by the author. Find out more about this organization at https://www.bbbs.org/

All people, locations, events, and situations are portrayed to the best of the author's memory. While all of the events described are true, many names and identifying details have been changed to protect the privacy of the people involved.

No part of this book may be reproduced, stored in a retrieval system, or transmitted by any means without the written permission of the author and publisher.

Regalo Press
New York • Nashville
regalopress.com

Published in the United States of America
1 2 3 4 5 6 7 8 9 10

For the girl who sees herself in these pages.
Who wishes so deeply that someone would see her.
You were all I saw, as I wrote it all down.

I wrote *Crushed* for you.

2/2/96

Dear Future Husband,

It's only been two minutes since I wrote to you, but I need to tell you something. I believe that Jonathon Taylor Thomas (Home Improvement) was put on this Earth for me. For me to marry I mean. But if you are not him, I understand! God said you were meant for me! I'm praying for you. I cry a lot about boys. They never seem to like me! I'm loud and abnoxious and seem to come across and annoying. I also call

February 2, 1996

Dear Future Husband,

It's only been two minutes since I wrote to you, but I need to tell you something.

I believe that Jonathan Taylor Thomas (*Home Improvement*) was put on this earth for me. For me to marry I mean. But if you are not him, I understand. God said you were meant for me.

I'm praying for you. I cry a lot about boys, they never seem to like me. I'm loud and obnoxious and seem to come across as annoying.

I love you so much and I don't even know you. I have to confess I still can't get JTT out of my mind, I don't know what it is though.

Love Your Future Wife,
Kiersten Lyons

Table of Contents

Foreword by Chris Carmack..ix
Author's Note..xiii

Part One: "The Heartbreak"
Chapter One: The Moment Everything Changed...............5
Chapter Two: God Is Rude.................................11
Chapter Three: God Is *Still* Rude 25
Chapter Four: If He Could Just See… 31
Chapter Five: The List...................................46
Chapter Six: Oh Sh*t, It's Real 61

Part Two: "The How Did I Get Here?"
Chapter Seven: I Love You. I Know. 75
Chapter Eight: Criss-Cross Applesauce....................80
Chapter Nine: He's Mean Because He Likes You! 88
Chapter Ten: Late Bloomer 97
Chapter Eleven: Status Update—Still a Late Bloomer 107
Chapter Twelve: Growing Up 112
Chapter Thirteen: La La Land 122
Chapter Fourteen: Losing Myself 141
Chapter Fifteen: California Dreaming.....................154

Part Three: "The Breakthrough"
Chapter Sixteen: Enough 167
Chapter Seventeen: Lowering the Red Flag 172

Chapter Eighteen: Raising the Green Flag 184

Chapter Nineteen: A Real-Life Romcom 191

Chapter Twenty: Bye Bye Bye 197

Chapter Twenty-One: The Sweetest Redemption............203

Chapter Twenty-Two: Big Sister 211

Chapter Twenty-Three: That Time I Challenged
        Taylor Swift 222

Chapter Twenty-Four: Hope 237

Chapter Twenty-Five: Dear You (Again) 241

Epilogue..244

Acknowledgments...248

About the Author 254

*foreword

by Chris Carmack ♡

I'm not a doctor...but I play one on TV.

Long before I played Atticus Lincoln on *Grey's Anatomy* or Luke Ward on *The O.C.*, I was a high school drama kid in Maryland trying to find my way in the world and just one high school away from the author of this book. My drama club and Kiersten's had a friendly rivalry, but it didn't stop us from showing up for each other's performances, traveling to theater festivals together, or doing our best Cabbage Patch at each other's homecoming dances. All of these moments were commemorated on Kodak cameras and in the backs of yearbooks. It was before the internet and cloud storage, so I don't know what has survived, but I'm told there will be pictures in this book, so I guess I'll find out the hard way. Through all of this, Kiersten kept me laughing. I'm sure an element of her comedy was forged in the fires of life, but as someone who knew her when, I say quite confidently she was a born comedian.

When we found ourselves both in a strange city three thousand miles from home in our early twenties, she con-

kiersten lyons

tinued to make me laugh. And our shared laughs may have been what got us through our formative years pounding the pavement on Hollywood's streets. I was there for a lot of the story she tells in this book. I'm not a main character, but I like to think I was bit of a touchstone for her, as she was for me. We reminded each other of who we were, where we came from, and our value, every time we got crushed in a city and industry that frankly didn't care whether we lived or died. That seems harsh, but it was true.

We left our families, and homes, and everything and everyone who did care about us to follow a dream. In this we were the same. There was endless opportunity for success but also endless opportunity to lose yourself or fall prey to those cottage industries that take advantage of fresh meat. We were the meat. In this too, we were the same. I needn't go into detail; she will in this book. We watched each other get crushed and rise again and again. I proudly watched her turn her pain into laughter and beauty when she mounted her one woman show, *Crushed*. I wish I could say it was smooth sailing for her after that, but there's no Hollywood endings in Hollywood. It wouldn't be the last time she was crushed, but it was a poignant moment when she took control of her own narrative and started winning a whole lot more. As a father myself now (and one who can't help but be terrified of how others will try to write my daughters' stories for them), I am once again proudly watching Kiersten spread a beautiful and hilarious message of empowerment.

Thank you, Kiersten, for continuing to be true to yourself and others. Still a touchstone. And to you, the reader…

crushed

also thank you. It is through your laughter that we heal, and through your lens that these stories are given meaning. And finally, to Jonathan Taylor Thomas, whom neither of us has ever met—you missed your chance, bro. She's married now.

author's note

Dear Reader,

I wrote this book for you. I mean, okay, if we're being technical, yes, I wrote the previous letter to my future husband when I was fourteen and a freshman in high school, hoping that someday, somewhere, *someone* would like me. And at the time, I was desperately hoping that person was Jonathan Taylor Thomas.

…And I'm now realizing you may not know who Jonathan Taylor Thomas is. Number one: *how dare you?!* And Number two: stop reading this book right now (I know my publisher just *loves* that I said that) and go watch season four of *Home Improvement*, the animated *Lion King*, and the cinematic masterpiece that is *Tom and Huck*.

In. That. Order.

Now that we're both on the same page about the genius and beauty of JTT (but also, like, step back; he's mine), you can understand how very devastating it was to learn he was, in fact, *not* put on this earth for me to marry. And therefore, I couldn't give those letters to him. But even more devastating? I couldn't give them to my *actual* fiancé either. Because two months before our wedding, while I was tying the bows

kiersten lyons

on our wedding invitations, he walked in to tell me he was pretty sure he didn't love me.

And maybe he never had.

In all my years of loving boys who didn't love me back, living in Los Angeles, struggling as an actress*, and being told I wasn't "pretty enough" (more on that later), I'd never known pain like this. I'd heard of people dying from heartbreak, and at the time, I was sure I would be next.

---

*It wasn't just letters to my future husband I was writing when I was a kid. I was also writing letters to select cast members of *Full House* (read: Jodie Sweetin) letting her know, yes, I was available to be on her show as a cousin who comes to live with the family, and of course, I would dye my hair blonde to fit in.

I'm still waiting to hear back from her.

But true to my word, I did dye my hair blonde once, but that was because I let a beauty school student give me highlights just before a big audition, and my hair turned orange, and the blonde was to fix it. I did book that job though—a guest star on TNT's *The Closer*, thankyouverymuch.

Turns out I almost did die, but not of heartbreak—of *heat stroke*. Because like anyone suffering from a called-off wedding would, I flew across the country to the home where I grew up and took my childhood bike out around the neighborhood man-made lake, a trail which I had forgotten was literally *miles* long. And apparently, riding around on a too-small-for-you bike and crying out literally every single ounce

crushed

of tears you have in 98 percent humidity can make you turn grey and almost pass out in the woods where no one would find you.

As I dry heaved in the bathroom of the neighborhood pool where I used to lifeguard as a teenager, I looked around, devastated. I had spent so many summers crying in this bathroom, so sure life would be better when I finally grew up. How had I ended up right back where I started, crying in a stall as families splashed outside, teen lifeguards flirted, and tweens used their babysitting money to order Domino's, completely unaware of my life falling apart on the other side of the wall?

Everyone's life was perfect (I mean, they were ordering Domino's!). From where I sat, it seemed I was the only one heartbroken. The only one struggling. The only one crushed.

It took me months to learn that wasn't true, and three years to fully believe it: everyone gets crushed. I don't want you to have to wait three years to understand that truth like I did. You are *not alone*. And knowing that is the first step to healing. The first step to knowing you are going to be okay.

It happened right after the first press preview of my one woman show, *Crushed: Why Is It That the Boys You Like, Never Like You Back?*

After ten years of acting in LA, my audition opportunities were still very few and far between because of the "You're not pretty enough" and the always popular "You're great; we just don't know what to do with you." Creating *Crushed* was me taking a page from every artist's playbook: I wrote and performed my own heartbreak. I just didn't realize my grief would help so many others to see their own.

"Thank you so much for your show. I really thought I was the only one."

It happened again the next night. And the next. Over and over. After each show, girls (and sometimes boys—you know, the ones without cooties) would come up laughing that a detail from my show so similarly mirrored their own life. Crying because they truly thought they were the only one in fourth grade who asked a boy out seven times and was rejected seven times. Hugging me because for the first time, they realized that someone else knew the pain of being so sure a boy was for them when he was surely not. Writing and performing *Crushed* ended up being the most healing thing for me in more ways than one. One night my favorite writer/producer just happened to come to the show (I didn't invite him, but he randomly came), and in a matter of days, we just happened to be sitting in his production offices on my favorite studio lot, mapping out the trajectory for *Crushed* and my career as he kept saying over and over:

"I know exactly what to do with your show."

I felt so seen.

FINALLY.

Until I wasn't.

Because what was on track to give me the break I had so deeply and abidingly worked toward in LA for over a decade was completely pulled out from under me. Promises that were made were broken—or maybe better described as vanished.

Because I got ghosted.

crushed

When the big writer/producer got the greenlight to direct his first feature, he became bigger, and I became a casualty of his success. And for all my time in LA, all the savvy I thought I had, I never once saw this coming...

But you know what else I didn't see coming? **YOU.**

What started out as people coming up after shows became texts, phone calls from friends of friends, and so many Facebook messages (don't judge—it was 2012, Facebook was cool, leave me alone). They had just gotten their wedding called off; would it be okay to talk because they didn't know anyone else who had gone through it? They lost their job; was I around to talk? Their niece didn't get into her dream college; could I chat? The realization that they weren't alone, coupled with seeing how freeing it was for me to tell the truth, gave each of them the courage to do the same.

When this book comes out, it will have been sixteen years since my ex first told me he didn't love me, thirteen since I created a show about it, and eleven since that producer ghosted me. It's been eleven since I first wrote the TV pilot version of *Crushed*, sending it and other scripts out to everyone I could think of, and hearing back the same, "We love it, but we really don't know what to do with it," several times over.

Ten years since a big entertainment literary agent wrote back, "I really love your work. When can I see the live show I've heard so much about?"

Ten since I put the whole thing up again at a theater in Hollywood for her. Ten since I sent out handmade press kits so that hopefully other industry people would come too. Ten

kiersten lyons

since she emailed me so excited about the *Crushed* slap bracelet in her press kit. Ten since I walked onstage to a packed house—save two seats. Because she never showed. And neither did any other agent or producer.

It's been ten years since I walked away from the industry that I was so sure would heal so much of my pain. Ten years since I tried everything I could think of to make my dreams come true.

Five years since I randomly learned that same agent now worked at the same agency my friend was with. Five since she said she remembered the slap bracelet I sent her in the handmade press kit I'd sent out. She never mentioned anything about not coming to the show she had asked me to put on, and instead she asked to read more of my stuff.

Five years since I sent her everything I had, including the TV pilot I had produced myself, just like *Crushed*. And it's been five since that friend texted me,

"It's not going to work out with _____, unfortunately. She said she wants to be 'holy shit' excited about someone new."

I got that text on my birthday.

Three years since I, ever so timidly, began to share *Crushed* on TikTok and someone commented:

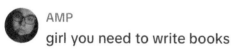

Three years since I thought, *I would love to, but it hurts too much to try again.*

crushed

And it's been two years since I read an article about teen girls experiencing extraordinarily high amounts of sadness and violence that changed everything. Minutes after finishing it, I turned on my iPhone's camera, looked into the lens, and said, "This message is for teenage girls."

I repeated the stats I had just read: "Sixty percent of teen girls are experiencing persistent sadness and hopelessness. Thirty percent have thought seriously of harming themselves, and ten percent have." I was crying and so blotchy from nerves, but I had to keep going. "I wish I would've had someone tell me it was going to be okay. Things that I just can't believe happened in my life—pivots and hardships and heartbreaks…so much heartbreak…that ended up being really, really, really good."

I thought of my little-girl self writing that letter to her future husband, so sure she knew exactly who he was. Telling him that boys didn't like her but holding hope that one day someone would.

"And I just want you to know you matter…whoever you are. Whatever you believe. Whoever you love. You matter."

I can't pretend the minute I uploaded it I didn't try to take it down. It felt so vulnerable, and seriously, I was *so blotchy*. I felt exposed, embarrassed. But before I could press delete, someone commented:

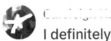

I definitely needed to hear this. I'm going through so much right now. Thank you

3-2 Reply   ♥ 16

kiersten lyons

And then,

It became clear that even though I made it for the sixteen-year-old watching on her phone, it was also for the sixteen-year-old that's still within each of us, who's still doing her best to hold hope when the world around her feels anything but hopeful. And she is worth being embarrassed for.

Two years and a month since I re-shared the beginnings of *Crushed*.

This time, instead of tucking these comments away, I allowed them to arm me as I reached out to a friend's book

crushed

agent, literally shaking as I pressed *Send*. She wrote back a while later that she wanted to meet and chose the day.

I stared at the meeting invite—May 17, 2023.

Literally fourteen years to the *day* from when my ex told me he didn't love me.

I liked her right away; she wasn't like a Hollywood agent and felt so much more real. Within weeks I sent over some chapters, and within a few days I received a reply: She loved my writing. I was funny and made her laugh, but I wasn't a huge name, and memoirs like I was writing are a hard sell. I'm not Tina Fey. I'm not Jennette McCurdy. The words got blurry as I tried to finish the email, but I didn't need to. It was everything I've heard since I moved to LA twenty-three years ago.

"You're great, but…"

Except this time, it's different. Because *Crushed* is different. Yes, it started as a way to process hurt, an opportunity for my talent to be seen, but it became so much more. *Crushed* is the opportunity for each of us to know how truly seen we are.

Plus, is there anything more poetic (or effing hilarious) than a book about rejection *getting rejected??*

So, I emailed the agent right back, thanking her for the kind words and her honesty, and then I linked TikTok after TikTok, no longer tucking those comments away.

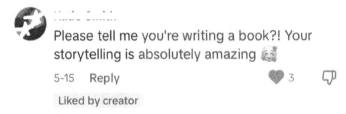

kiersten lyons

But as I checked to make sure the email I had sent actually went through (why, yes, I do have anxiety, thank you for asking), I was struck with how powerful the screen full of comments staring back was. I just *knew* she would finally see it.

But she didn't.

I won't pretend the entire process of this book hasn't been gut wrenching—from living it, to writing it, to finding an

crushed

agent who truly got it, to finally being sent out to publishers and getting crushed all over again: "She's great, but…"

No, but really—over and over and *over* again. I won't pretend it didn't cause tears and confusion and more than once asking myself if it was all worth it. But then I would get a message from someone like you.

kiersten lyons

It was worth it because *you're* worth it.
And so is she.

She's sixteen and doing her best to cling to hope as she is called names and made fun of for her chicken legs and flat chest in her one-piece swimsuit. She's so sure that once she's famous, once she's on Broadway, they'll see that they were so wrong about her.

If she can only prove that to them, then maybe she'll believe it herself. She's still writing letters to her future husband, but this time she's so sure it's a boy she actually knows. He's funny, kind to his little sister, and so cute. Not like "high school boy" cute, like, "in three years he's going to be the face of Abercrombie, and girls will have his bag all over their rooms," cute. He also does theater too, at another school where it's cooler to be a theater kid. He laughs at her jokes, and when she asks him to her school's homecoming as friends, he accepts, even bringing her a rose corsage. She's so sure soon he'll see her as more than a friend.

crushed

But he never does, because life doesn't always go the way you planned. We get crushed, we get heartbroken, and we also get surprised. Because the boy that sixteen-year-old me was so sure she was going to marry?

He wrote the foreword you just read.

And the letter I wrote to my future husband? The one where I was crying about boys not liking me because I was annoying and loud? The one where I was so sad? Well, that day, that *exact* date, February 2, 1996, would become one of the greatest days of my life—I just didn't know it yet.

You've probably surmised by now (I mean, you're literally holding the book) a publisher did see the book, see me… see us. In fact, I signed the book deal May 17, 2024. Fifteen years to the day my ex told me he didn't love me.

Sixteen-year-old me had dreams of her memoir, filled with glamorous tales of Hollywood sets and torrid affairs, and yet this one is so much better. Because it's real and really surprising. I will never *not* be in awe of the twists and turns it took to get here.

I don't know what life has in store for you, but I know one day you're going to look at a picture of yourself from right now and be so excited to tell her about all the surprises she has to look forward to.

Julianna
your account is like a hug from the version of myself i hope to meet in the future. thank you

5-16   Reply   2

Liked by creator

kiersten lyons

You're going to be okay. Actually, better than okay. And until you're there, I'll be right here, sitting beside you with that non-dairy ice cream.

Or dairy, if you're able, but you don't have to brag about it.

part one

"THE HEARTBREAK"

THE TAYLOR SWIFT
"WHITE HORSE" OF IT ALL...

Look, there are going to be moments (like literally the previous page) when I reference a song, because it's either the theme for the section or because the lyrics are kind of essential. Also, "kind of essential" is my family paying our electric bill, so as much as I would like to have secured the music rights to have all of these lyrics on page for you, I don't have that kind of money. And I don't know if you've been following along thus far, but we don't always get what we want...like me never having a boyfriend during my formative years that I could make a CD mix for.

But you know what's better than a mixed CD for a teenage boy with a not-yet-fully-formed frontal lobe to appreciate said thoughtful gift? A carefully curated Spotify playlist for you that at any point during this book you can refer to:

kierstenlyons.com/crushedthebook

Please also use for crying in the shower, crying in your car, or the ever-popular crying on the airplane on your way back to your hometown as you look down at all the tiny houses and think to yourself, *all these people have perfect lives, and I'm the only one silently sobbing into my neck pillow because my life is completely over!*

Oh, just me?

kiersten lyons

Also, for your reference, I've created a timeline for the "White Horse" portion of my life, because we all know heartbreak often means one moment might trigger a memory, which might trigger a thousand more. Because that is grief. And while grief isn't linear, history very much is.

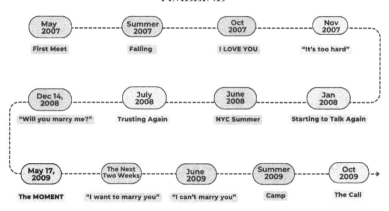

Chapter One ♡

the moment everything changed

MAY 17, 2009

> *Roses are Red,*
> *Violets are Blue,*
> *The sex was amazing last night,*
> *Let's do this again soon.*
> *—Jessica*

> *I can't believe I just met you 13 hours ago…and*
> *by the way your shower IS really roomy…*
> *—Tanya*

> *I loved you in the Outback commercial, and*
> *inside me…*
> *—Sarah*

How had I become that girl? You know, the girl on the verge of marrying a guy who has a chalkboard-painted bathroom graffitied with notes from former one-night stands that he just couldn't erase because it was "part of who he was"?

kiersten lyons

I say verge because roughly seven minutes before this, I was sitting on his bed, blissfully tying the bows on our wedding invitations. James walked in and sat in his wooden desk chair. The chair turned ever so slightly as he ran his fingers through his hair. I'm pretty sure he was auditioning for the opening credits of *90210*.

"I don't think I love you."

My hands immediately stopped tying.

"How long have you been feeling this?"

"I dunno."

I was calm. This wasn't new territory for him, for us, so there was no cause for alarm. Looking back now, it alarms me how much this didn't alarm me.

"I don't think I know what love is."

I asked again, "How long have you been feeling this?"

"Why do you keep asking me that?"

The satin ribbon pulled tight in my hands. "Did you cheat on me?"

This also wasn't new territory for him.

"Why would you ask me that?" he fired back. "I need to talk to my sister. She's the only one who gets me."

And then he walked out and disappeared for the next forty-five minutes.

I looked down at the invitation. The ribbon was cutting off my circulation. I just couldn't let go. Then I had no choice—I felt the immediate urge to be sick. I ran into that bathroom only to be confronted by all those girls on the walls.

Last night was great. Let's do IT again soon.
—Catherine

crushed

I ran back to his room, searching for the box I had brought over just days before. The day I put my entire life in storage. My entire life except my bed, which I had gifted to a newly divorced dad who had answered my Craigslist ad in the "For Free" section. I specifically remember watching the dad take it down my West Hollywood stairs and thinking, "The next bed I sleep in will be our bed—the bed my future husband and I are picking out together."

I was crashing on my friend Sage's couch for the two months leading up to our wedding because I'd decided I wasn't living with anyone until marriage. That was peculiar to James; he'd lived with an ex-girlfriend, maybe two. He'd also slept with a large percentage of Manhattan and Los Angeles, so my lack of living and sleeping with him wasn't just *peculiar*—it was downright *terrible* for him.

But I was worth it. That's what he'd said.

I found my journal at the bottom of the box, maybe the twelfth one I'd had since moving to LA to pursue my dreams of being famous. I mean, acting. Well, both.

Twenty minutes passed without him coming back. I scribbled furiously, telling God I wanted to marry a man who loved me. Who really loved me, sacrificially. Who, before he'd ever hurt me, would care more about his relationship with God than his relationship with me. Who loved me.

James still wasn't back.

I walked through the house, passing his roommate's door. The roommate who didn't like me because I wasn't hot enough for James. Something he told James, and something James told me.

kiersten lyons

I found James out on the balcony and on the phone.

"She's here. I have to go."

I heard his sister say goodbye. He looked at me angry, like I had done something wrong.

I don't know how long we were out there before I asked the question again, but something told me to. "Did you cheat on me?"

He shook his head no but wouldn't meet my eyes. No *90210* opening credits this time.

Again, something nagged me to ask once more. James shifted his weight in the chair, so annoyed with my questioning. "Yeah. Fine. Is that what you wanted to hear?"

That was the last thing I wanted to hear. I asked him when, as if the timeline could somehow ease the knot that was forming in my stomach. Was it before or after he proposed? He mumbled something about his work Christmas party. My brain scanned dates, trying to figure out when exactly that was, but everything felt foggy, fuzzy. I asked him when that was, and he countered that it was months ago; how could he remember the exact date?

"Let me see your phone. I want to look in your calendar."

The minute I said this, his entire face fell, because he already knew. It was December 15, 2008, the night after he proposed to me on the balcony of the Chateau Marmont.

The Chateau Marmont. Don't worry, he cheated at the Magic Castle.

The. Magic. Castle.

For those of you who don't know, the Magic Castle was a members-only home shaped like a castle in the Hollywood

crushed

Hills where they did…magic. I'm pretty sure Neil Patrick Harris was an owner at one point. What I'm saying is, when one thinks of places where inhibitions run wild, it's most definitely a fake castle where Doogie Howser is performing magic.

I hit him. James, not Doogie. On his chest, over and over. At one point I felt myself float up above and watch this drama play out. It all felt very *Dawson's Creek*, and as much as I wanted to be on that show, I did not want to be *in* that show.

> The original *Doogie Howser, M.D.* was a TV sitcom that ran from 1989 to 1993 about a genius teen doctor, played by Neil Patrick Harris. NPH would go on to even bigger fame for playing Barney Stinson in *How I Met Your Mother*, but I think calling him Doogie Howser in this context is funnier, and I'm the writer, so I get to make these decisions.

My hits were pathetic and offered no relief. I remember taking off my engagement ring and throwing it at him. It was Tiffany's, a solitaire, and everything I thought I wanted. I remember him telling me he did love me and staring at the street below, the same street that every morning hundreds of cars would crawl across trying to get a parking space to hike Runyon Canyon.

He saw the girl he had lived with there one time. It was before me, but years after they had spoken. He had cheated on her too. He had cheated on every single girl he'd ever been with. It made sense—so had his father. His father had married the woman he cheated on James's mother with, and then

kiersten lyons

he cheated on that woman, too. I didn't so much understand generational wounds just yet, but I did understand romcoms.

James was the guy all the girls wanted, the witty and handsome guy (he was a model, for goodness' sake) who never had a real man to model his life after. He'd never known real love, the kind of love that is unconditional and loves you down to your very soul. I didn't fall for his lines like the girls that came before me. In fact, the first night I met him, the beautiful bartender working alongside him at Bar Marmont looked at me with a smirk and said, "James, watch out for this one. She's different than the rest."

It was everything I had always wanted.

Chapter Two

God is rude

If you've ever been to a twelve-step meeting or, I don't know, just listened to a mere eight minutes of Dax Shepard's *Armchair Expert*, you've heard the term *higher power*. For some, it's the universe; for others, it's nature. For me, it's God.

From the moment I entered my first Al-Anon meeting, I came face-to-face with story after story of gut-wrenching heartbreak, deep longing, and prayers going anyway but the way we want.

I walked into the meeting not sure if I should even be there, but within minutes I realized I was exactly in the right spot. I was starting to see how worried I often was about James's drinking—always worried about how much he was consuming when I wasn't around and the choices that would come out of it.

Like, you know, cheating on his fiancé the night after he proposed.

kiersten lyons

> Per their website: Al-Anon is for people who are worried about someone with a drinking problem. It offers community, tools, and the twelve-step program to help those cope and accept the things they can't change.

But it was more than James: as I heard story after story of loved ones' heartbreak, I realized how universal it was to try to change others. How human it was to wrestle with our obvious lack of control.

From infancy, we are told if we believe it, we can achieve it—if we pray hard enough, the door will open. And yet, no matter what any of us did, our higher power was all, "NOPE!"

Rude.

I wasn't just writing letters *about* Jonathan Taylor Thomas; I wrote letters *to* him as well. It's at this point I should confess James is not the only one who's lied to a romantic partner. I was given a *Nickelodeon Magazine* with Jonathan Taylor Thomas on the cover (look, I know it's easier to write JTT, but he has expressed in many interviews that he doesn't like that moniker, and I will respect him until the day I die). Anyway, I received this magazine, and in it, he talked of his future plans to go to college at Northwestern, to possibly study directing, and said that his favorite cheese was gouda. I promptly wrote him a letter. I asked him if he had, in fact, read the dystopian tween novel *The Giver*, because I thought he would love it. This was not the lie. I had read it a few times (it was on my summer reading list) and loved it. I knew if I brought it up, he would be impressed. I was so sure most girls were writing to him about the *Sweet Valley High* book series or other such nonsense. I also told him my favorite cheese was gouda.

crushed

It's at this moment I should note I am allergic to dairy and at that point in my life had never tried nor even seen gouda. In that moment I created myself to be who I thought the person I loved would love back. It wouldn't be the last time.

Forget the hundreds of thousands of prayers where I'd *begged* God to let me marry Jonathan Taylor Thomas, to get the part in the school play I wanted, for Jodie Sweetin to finally answer my letter back where I detailed that I would most definitely dye my hair blonde so I could play a cousin, or, I don't know…*MAYBE NOT HAVE MY WEDDING CALLED OFF?!?!*

All those solid nos.

But every time I'm all, "Your will be done," then God's like, "I got you."

So. Rude.

God *never* gives me what I want unless it is good for me, and honestly, that is not only *rude*, but it also makes having plans pretty much impossible.

You know—like wedding plans.

James was raised with money—like, penthouse-in-the-city-and-a-home-in-Tuxedo-Park kind of money. Yes, you read that right: Tuxedo Park. And why is it called that? Because it was where the term for the fanciest of men's formalwear was coined.

kiersten lyons

I, on the other hand, was raised with two brothers and two sisters, parceling out one large McDonald's french fry between five of us. No, literally: we would count them out one-by-one, and whoever got to sit in the front seat on the way home from the drive-thru usually snuck extras. For years that honor belonged to my older brother, but one day he moved on from riding with the family, and it became my job sit up front and hold the bag of dinner. As much of a people pleaser as I was (the consummate goodie-two-shoes who was always chosen by the teacher to "watch the class" if they had to run out), I felt absolutely no remorse for taking an extra handful of fries.

James had absolutely no remorse for taking an extra handful of women. Actually, I take that back; he felt tons of remorse—shame, in fact—but he covered it up with anger (that he took out on me) because I dared to desire someone who loved me well.

We had broken up once before, days after the night I first met his father. You know, the father who owned the house in Tuxedo Park. The father who cheated on his mother (and then married the woman he cheated with, and then cheated on her).

The father that taught his son to keep secrets.

JUNE 2007

The Little Door is a farm-to-table restaurant that caters to LA's elite. It's where James and I had our first real date, and it's the first time I experienced James's incredible ability to lie. It was a busy night, the kind of night where every time the

crushed

door opens the entire place looks up to see who walked in and judge if they were famous or beautiful (or both).

James was the latter; he was categorically beautiful. I was the eternal late bloomer consistently told I "wasn't pretty enough" by casting directors, producers, and, as we all know, his roommate. Couple this with a childhood filled with words like "ugly" and "gross" being tossed my way, and I was equal parts enamored with this beautiful person taking me out and uncomfortable with the whole thing too. Everyone turned as we made our way to the host stand. A beautiful girl looked for our name but couldn't seem to find it.

"Really? Amos said he called it in. Huh...."

"Amos?"

"Yeah, Amos McArthur."

Her eyes widened at the name.

"Let me just text him quick. He's so busy, I really should've reminded him.... It's my fault."

"No, no. It's completely fine. You don't need to do that." She winked, grabbing two menus and showed us to a cozy two top. I asked James who Amos was.

"He's the owner of a few places I've worked at, and I definitely didn't call him."

He nestled into his menu, so pleased with himself. I learned later that Amos did, in fact, have a soft spot for James. Apparently, he loved hiring charming guys who could get any girl they wanted. It made his establishments that much more desirable and in turn made *him* desirable.

To be fair, we're talking about LA. There exists a catering company called Beautiful Bartenders, and applying for a waitress job often means little clothing and lots of flirting. Sex sells—or the allusion of it at least—and the power of knowing you could with anyone at any time could be intoxicating.

OCTOBER 2007

The Little Door was quieter the night I met James's father—maybe a Monday, but I can't remember exactly. That's the thing about heartbreak: some things are so vivid, others fuzzy. James's face as we walked in is still vivid in my memories. He gripped my hand with this nervous excitement I hadn't seen before, almost childlike, so excited to show his dad the girl that was so different than the rest. I loved when he said that. He also said that the guy who would be joining his father was a shark, "so get ready."

But the guy wasn't a shark—he was just an older married finance bro hitting on our server at a farm-to-table restaurant. So…typical. James's dad? He was right there with him, but the flirting was all the more effortless with him.

He ordered for the table: a charcuterie board, my first one. Don't get me wrong; I'd had a Lunchables before (I'm not a monster), but this wooden cutting board filled with a hundred dollars' worth of meats and cheeses was completely out of my league. James's dad regaled us with each cheese and why he chose them: "And this gouda pairs nicely with—"

My eyes narrowed in on the elusive cheese.

Who was I to judge this father who had lied so much when I too had lied to Jonathan? It was time to make myself an honest woman and try it—the gouda—dairy issues and

crushed

all. Spoiler alert: Lactaid pills and expensive wine do not pair well, and I spent most of later that night curled up in a ball.

NOVEMBER 2007

James and I were sitting outside the Coffee Bean & Tea Leaf on Sunset deep in West Hollywood, chatting about the night with his dad. He saw that I saw right through his dad, and he loved that about me (and I loved that he loved that).

I sipped a tea latte. It was cold that night (well, cold for LA), and my throat was a little sore, but I didn't care. I would have sat outside in a tundra if it meant James being this open.

He watched the cars rounding the corner on Sunset. "I can't explain it, but being with you has made me realize every single one of my past relationships has mirrored my dad's."

He kept looking out at the cars, talking and processing, almost as if he forgot I was there. I put my hand over his. It jolted him back to reality; he stopped talking, fear in his eyes. There was that little boy face again, as if he wanted me to ask him something to relieve the guilt but also was begging me not to. I studied his face, knowing I needed to gently ask, "Has our relationship mirrored it?"

He was so vulnerable talking about his dad, and I knew he was trying to overcome a lot. My dad also had to overcome a lot when it came to masculinity, and so, like I would dozens of other times over the course of our relationship, I took myself out of the equation. I asked again.

It turns out right after we became exclusive, he went on an actors' retreat with a bunch of former and current NYU

kiersten lyons

students. It was all very creative (read: weird), as those things are, and one night, lit by only a campfire, he kissed another girl. She was nineteen, barely out of her freshman year of college, and had been following him around that week. I knew this because he had already told me about her—just not the kissing part.

I got quiet, still partially out of the equation, as I saw him look at me. There was that childhood face again.

"I don't want to be my dad. I don't want to keep secrets from you."

I picked up his hand and held it tightly. I told him it was just a kiss, months before, and I forgave him.

"You forgive me?"

I nodded, and he pulled me in, tears in his eyes. We had already said "I love you" just a week earlier, but this time felt it deeper. More real.

Which made what happened two nights later that much worse.

He called me from his car minutes after his shift had ended. It was eleven or so, and it had been slow at Bar Marmont. Days after we became exclusive, I'd given him my guest parking pass—a coveted gift that allowed him to park just behind my apartment, a mere two blocks from the Chateau. It would save him so much time searching the Hollywood Hills for parking, save him so much money parking in a lot (which, looking back, the kid had a trust fund—he didn't need it). Either way, I loved giving it to him because it meant many nights I could race down in my pjs already, sometimes half asleep, to kiss him goodnight. This night felt no different—until I got into the car and saw his face.

crushed

Gone was the childlike grin. In its place, a cold stare filled with anger. So much anger.

"We're too different. This is too much."

I felt as if the wind was knocked out of me as his voice raised, yelling about sex and our lack thereof. Which was confusing, because just after he'd confessed to kissing that girl, just after I had forgiven him, he'd looked into my eyes and told me that as hard as it had been to not have sex, he realized how strong it made our communication, our relationship, because he wasn't blinded by it at all.

"But two days ago, you said—"

He cut me off, furious that I would use his words against him.

"I'm not using your words against you; I just don't understand. You told me you loved that about me. You loved me."

"Well, maybe I was wrong."

By this time, I was sobbing and somehow curling myself into a ball on his passenger seat. He refused to look at me.

I don't remember how I got into my friend Skylar's car, or even when I called him, but I soon found myself so grateful for the extra twin mattress he had in his studio apartment. So grateful not to be alone.

Four hours later I was up, eyes wide, staring at the ceiling. Nights aren't my issue with breakups—it's the morning. The moment you wake up and suddenly realize it isn't a bad dream, and suddenly you can't find your breath.

And it was definitely morning, maybe 4 a.m., and as much as I tried to will myself to fall back asleep, I couldn't. Everything James had ever said or did swirled through my

kiersten lyons

mind, each moment more painful (and confusing) than the last. Where was that stupid gouda with the Lactaid and wine? That pain I could take.

My mind wasn't the only thing buzzing; my body was aching to move, so sure that would make the swirling thoughts calm. I quietly got up, scribbled a note to Skylar letting him know I was walking home (not kidnapped, as I was sure he would think), and walked out. It was still dark out as I trudged up La Brea Ave, just above 4th Street, and made (what I realize now was) the three-mile trek to my place off Sunset. I couldn't walk fast enough, so sure the quick pace would somehow ease the pain. I crossed over Santa Monica and up Fairfax until I came face to face with the last place I wanted to see: a Catholic church.

RUDE.

He was in there—you know, the irritating One—but I had nothing to say to Him. He was the reason I was in such pain. I believed in Him, so James now didn't believe in *us*.

Yet before I knew it, I was pulling at the massive doors trying to get in. Which was futile. It was barely 5 a.m. No one was in there, but I kept pulling, trying to will those stupid doors to open.

Fine, whatever. I didn't want in there anyway.

I turned back to the street, tears rolling down my cheeks, and then, with the same force that caused me to start this stupid expedition, my body pivoted back. I had to get in.

I had to put this pain, this rejection, this ultimate failure *somewhere*, and for whatever reason, this seemed like the most

crushed

logical place. That only made me angrier, my tears hotter. I tried a side door: locked. Then another: locked too.

I thought you said, "Knock and the door will open?!"

Just then, a small door appeared. I mean, not like magically with fairy dust—I just noticed one I hadn't seen before. I yanked at it in anger, and it flung open.

Oh, sure, now You care.

The inside was dark, lit by a few candles underneath a statue. The minute the door shut, I let out a cry I can only describe as guttural, the pain so deep. It didn't stop. It had very much settled in me. Somehow, I knew it was being witnessed (if nothing else by the statues), and that gave me some teeny, tiny sense of comfort. I scowled at the candles, some tall, some barely holding on, but all signifying a soul asking, yearning, hoping…

What's the use?

And yet, not thirty seconds later, I was begging. Crying those tears that fall down your face so fast that you can barely breathe but breathing just enough to let God know how hurt I was. A flame flickered under a saint that had the same real name as James, and I stared at it, quietly asking the saint, asking God, to help James see he deserved more than he was allowing himself.

JANUARY 2008

"I'm realizing my mom never forgave my dad."

We were back in his car, getting back together. It was two months after he told me maybe he didn't love me, two months

kiersten lyons

after my crying (okay, wailing) episode in the dark church, two months after he had told me about kissing that girl.

Except it wasn't just a kiss with that nineteen-year-old.

They'd slept together, and when I had forgiven him so quickly for the kiss, he shame-spiraled, leading him to bubble over with anger at my ability to forgive what was only half the truth. Couple that with the fact that everyone around him thought it odd he was dating a girl who wouldn't sleep with him until marriage (but had slept with her first boyfriend—more on that later), and it had all been too much. We talked and talked and talked some more. He leaned in to kiss me one night; was that the way he leaned into the nineteen-year-old?

We spent the next week talking in that car. Late nights filled with confessions and secrets exposed. At one point he handed me a stack of journals dating back a decade and a tiny glass vial.

"I want you, I want us, and I don't want these secrets."

I looked down at the journals, touched that he would share them with me but also wary. This was a big change in such a short time. I rolled the glass vial in between my fingers, unsure what it was. Turns out it was for cocaine: he was done with his old life, he assured me, and offered these as a symbol.

His sister was in town, and he desperately wanted me to meet her, and I desperately wanted to trust him again. I looked at the journal, opening the cover. His familiar handwriting filled the first page. I flipped to a random page in the middle. It was an entry from his first serious relationship,

crushed

the girl he'd lived with, the girl he saw once hiking Runyan Canyon, the first girl he ever cheated on. I skipped down: they were broken up, but still living together trying to work it out when she hadn't come home. The page was filled with pain, him realizing what he did and how she was moving on.

I looked up at him, at his now-familiar boyish expression, vulnerable in sharing his past, excited about the future. Excited about us.

"I've never been loved unconditionally, and that scared me, so I ran. But I'm not scared anymore. I love you, and I promise I'm not going anywhere." He eyed the open journal. "I promise I'm done running."

I met his sister a couple nights later. She was vibrant and funny, and I liked her right away. She watched James and I banter back and forth, nodding her approval. Over the next few months that nod would come often as I met more friends and family. Each couldn't believe this girl who believed in God was so funny.

JUNE 2008

"How can I be a better father?"

It was the following summer. James and I were back together in Manhattan having lunch at his dad's favorite little spot.

At that moment, James was on the phone with his younger half-brother (the younger half-brother his dad ignored most days because he wasn't good at sports) when he overheard his dad ask me this. James knew I wouldn't tiptoe around; his

kiersten lyons

father had been such a topic in our relationship, and I wasn't going to let him off the hook just because everyone else did.

"Do you want me to tell you the truth or what you want to hear?"

James's face registered panic as his father assured me, he wanted the truth.

I leaned in. "Stop keeping secrets, because you aren't fooling anyone."

I said more, but that's the line that made James almost choke on the extremely expensive lunch his dad was treating us to.

Even with his all secrets, I liked James's dad. I had compassion for James's father's upbringing and why he had made some of the choices he made. I loved James's stepmom. The younger brother James had been on the phone with. Goodness, I cared about that little guy so much. His other younger half-brother, too. James's mom? Well, that was complicated, and not because of the typical soon-to-be mother-in-law stuff, but more so because we both loved Jesus.

Yup. You read that right. Apparently, the fact that she loved Jesus and was sleeping with her boyfriend, and I loved Jesus and wasn't sleeping with her son made her angry. Furious over it. Even though we literally never spoke about the topic once.

See, I told you—He's rude.

Chapter Three

God is *still* rude

So that night when I was tying the bows on our wedding invitations, that night when he told me he didn't think he knew what love was and that he needed to call his sister, that night when he finally confessed that he'd cheated again, it all made sense. This wasn't new territory.

We'd been here before; we'd gotten through it before.

I spent that night restless on Sage's couch. She lived a half a block from James. And the next morning, he called me to come back over. This time, he was the one sitting on the bed, and I was the one standing. He looked at me, his boyish charm holding my gaze as he told me he did love me, he wanted to marry me, and he just needed time and space to figure it all out.

And somehow, that made sense too.

I left for Laguna Beach (no, not the hit MTV show—the actual town) a week later.

MEMORIAL DAY WEEKEND 2009

Since January I had been a nanny for a sweet family with a six-year-old girl and three-year-old boy. Each Memorial

kiersten lyons

Day weekend they would head down to a stunning resort in Orange County. This place was somewhere I'm sure James and his family would've visited, and none of this was lost on me—what was lost was *sleep*. Maybe it was the incredibly uncomfortable pull-out couch (which made no sense as the suites were going for two grand a night), or the fact I hadn't talked to my fiancé in almost a week, but whatever it was, I was exhausted.

But then he called me.

The kids and I had been spending the last hour on a treasure hunt of sorts, following the bunnies that lived on property throughout the gardens and winding paths, when my phone rang with James's number. My heart leapt, but I was working, and I couldn't pick up. I waited breathlessly for a voicemail, only to be met with a text:

By mistake called you. Didn't mean to.

I texted back immediately. I miss you.

There was a third child with us—tagging along on our bunny adventure. She was the daughter of a TV star, although I didn't know it at the time because he wasn't with her on holiday. Like many powerful men, he didn't see the use in spending time with his family. He also didn't see the use in spending time treating others well. I know this because he's the only actor I've ever worked with that was truly cruel. He hadn't liked that I was making the crew laugh when I arrived on set one day. Minutes later, early into the shoot, I flubbed a line, and he took full advantage.

"You really stepped in it this time, little girl," he sneered.

crushed

I was twenty-six. I was not a little girl, and yet, in that moment, I felt so small. The entire set looked away from me ashamed. They'd seen this behavior before, but he was the star—what could they do? I had felt so powerless.

I looked back at James's text. So powerless.

The bunnies ended up hopping into the tall grass to be alone. I wanted to join them. Instead, I turned around and got smacked in the face with a large feather plume.

Yes, you read that right.

"The bride wants this at the top of the aisle."

Bride...?

All at once, it seemed an entire wedding appeared before us: stacks of gold Chivari chairs floated past, a large arch of roses, and more feathers marched beside the kids and me. Just at that moment, my boss, Emmy, walked up.

I went into that weekend determined to hide what was happening with James and me, but I lasted maybe thirty minutes before Emmy figured something was up. She now watched me watching the wedding set go by and sweetly nodded her head up towards the room. I shook my head, knowing I couldn't be trusted with my phone.

I stared down at it. My sent "I miss you" stared back with no reply.

We all had an early dinner by the pool. I had my usual nanny meal of chicken quesadilla and a Coke with a lime. I could've ordered something fancier—the family always sweetly told me to get whatever I wanted—but I never felt like I could. I would always be a parcel-out-the-McDonald's-french-fries kind of girl.

kiersten lyons

At this point, there was no escaping the wedding—light entrance music was playing as guests found their seats just below the pool balcony. All the families we were with had crowded at the edge to watch, each guessing the price of this affair. Most put it at $300,000.

Our wedding was going to maybe be one-twentieth of that. I kept trying to keep costs down, but James's father was all, "Get whatever you want." Now, as the wedding music swirled, "Get whatever you want," took on new meaning. People like James and his father, like that rich, cruel TV actor, got whatever they wanted. People like me didn't.

My eyes focused on the feather plumes (which had multiplied since I last saw them) when the music suddenly changed, and the groom appeared just in front of them. He was purposeful, not hiding or second guessing, but standing there confidently with this huge grin on his face. Those stupid feathers danced behind him in the wind, taunting me like, "You'll never have this. Nanny nanny boo boo."

I looked at Emmy beside me, and before I could say a thing, she gently nodded toward the beach with the softest smile. I nodded thanks and rushed out.

The resort was on a bluff, with these winding stairs made of boulders leading to the beach. Happy, wealthy, sun-kissed families coming back up to the hotel noticed the girl with tear-stained cheeks and whispered to each other.

I was whispering too.

"How could you do this, God? A wedding? How terrible are you?!"

crushed

I could hear the wedding march beginning—*how are there so many boulders?!*—and then I hit the sand, the sound of waves hiding the wedding away. The sounds of true love were replaced with the crashing tide coming in. It was so— *wait, what's that clicking sound?*

Click. Click.

I turned towards the ocean only to see a man on one knee as a girl held her face to her hands.

I was in the middle of a surprise engagement shoot.

Are you kidding me?! I screamed silently to God as I rushed past, staring at my feet moving through the sand. This was without a doubt the *rudest* th—

Click. Click.

I looked up from the sand to see *another* photographer. He was crouching down in a wade pool grabbing the perfect shot of—

ANOTHER ENGAGEMENT SHOOT?!?!

Over the years I've had so many people asked me how I kept faith during that time, and the answer is simple.

I didn't.

I bought a book at one point titled *May I Hate God?* I'm pretty sure I did, in fact, hate Him. But He had surprises waiting, moments that would cover over these days, that exact weekend, and the actual date May 17, with such redemption that I'm still in awe.

But don't get it twisted; I can be in awe and still think my higher power is rude. But more than rude, hilarious. Because I'm a comedy writer, and I'm not sure there is anything funnier than a girl in the midst of

kiersten lyons

getting her wedding called off, running away from a random wedding and into an engagement shoot.

Excuse me, *two* engagement shoots.

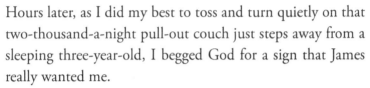

Hours later, as I did my best to toss and turn quietly on that two-thousand-a-night pull-out couch just steps away from a sleeping three-year-old, I begged God for a sign that James really wanted me.

I looked at my phone. It was 5 a.m., and he still hadn't texted. When he asked for space, I told him I could respect that if he could respect the fact that I still needed a text once he got home from his shift each night. He now worked at The Edison. It was downtown and the newest hot spot in LA—categorically beautiful people in all the categorically beautiful dimly lit corners.

I typed furiously, tears streaming down my face.

After everything, you can't even send me a text?!

And then he did.

I can't marry you.

Chapter Four

if he could just see...

"**B**aby, I'm going to marry you."

James was calling our wedding back on again.

Yes, you read that right...again.

He had just picked me up at the resort, less than twenty-four hours since he'd texted me it was off. Exactly a week since he called it off the first time on his balcony.

How had it only been a week?

I looked out the passenger window of his beloved Audi. The Audi that his father's trust fund paid for. You know, the father that James swore he didn't want to be like, and yet...

"Baby, you have to understand—I'm not sure I can make this kind of commitment."

I wish I could tell you that, when he said this, I looked at him and said, "You're right, you can't. I deserve more."

That I said *anything*.

But I couldn't. I was literally rendered speechless, because the minute I looked up at his stupid face, that ridiculously perfect boyish charm was looking back. Any time it surfaced, I was weak, powerless even, and not because he was so hand-

kiersten lyons

some (which he was—remember, *model* pretty), but because in those moments, that face registered all that he'd lost as a child and all that we'd found together.

JUNE 2007

"I have a surprise for you."

We were just starting to see each other, having only gone out a handful of times, and I was excited thinking he'd brought me a treat from The Chateau. The pastry chef there made a boozy ice cream that was especially perfect (even though it made my stomach hurt), and so I rushed outside with a spoon only to find him sitting in a brand-new Audi A4 with the top down, grinning from ear to ear, boyish-charm style.

"I kept seeing these around town, and I really wanted one, so I turned in my lease and got it."

I tried to look excited for him (and not super disappointed that there was no ice cream), but in truth, I'm not a fan of convertibles. They seem super cool until a strand of hair gets out of your ponytail and starts to whip your eye at sixty-five miles per hour. James thought he was a great driver but in truth was terrible (having been a city kid and only gotten his license a couple of years before), and the thought of less material between me and the road did not seem like the adventure I was after. Plus, the fact that he just liked something and got it, especially a luxury car, didn't impress me—it concerned me.

He registered my expression. "You don't like it?"

I looked at him. It really had only been a few weeks; how honest could I be?

crushed

I took a breath, choosing my words carefully. "I love that you love it, and you're so excited about it, but…"

His sweet grin was still there, letting me know I could keep going.

"It's not really my thing. There's a part of me that's concerned that you just like something and you get it, just like that. Also, I don't like leather seats. They're hot and sticky in the sun—I know they're like luxury, but just because someone tells us something is luxury doesn't mean it is…. I don't want what's cool—I want the best. I sold myself short for too long with trying to be cool, and now I just want what's best. I want…um…I want greatness."

Unexpectedly, he leaned in, holding my face in his hands. "You're not like anyone I've ever met."

MEMORIAL DAY WEEKEND 2009

"Why can't you understand how hard this is for me? I don't know anyone like you. You're not like my friends or family or anyone I've ever met. I'm doing my best!"

Now, almost two years later, sitting in that same car, those words felt accusatory, like something he was trying so hard to get over, so we could get on with it. *It* being the wedding. The marriage. You know, the *spending our whole lives together* part.

"Kiersten, we just drove a priest wearing a wool robe and Jesus sandals to the airport!"

"We got a beer first, and you said you liked him."

"I did, but it's still weird!"

I mean, he wasn't wrong. If I wasn't like most girls, then Father Diego was definitely not like most priests. I first met

kiersten lyons

him because a friend of mine dragged me to where he was performing spoken word in Hollywood (yes, you read that right). He was funny and blunt and lived in the Bronx—all things I knew James would appreciate.

They didn't meet until that drive, one Father told me years later was the most awkward drive of his life, to which I said:

"Oh, I'm sorry that the drive, mere hours after my fiancé called off our wedding via text, was awkward for *you!*"

Father Diego hung his head, laughing.

Because here's the thing: a few texts after James called off our wedding, I still had to ask him what I was supposed to do that afternoon. Why, may you ask? Because he was supposed to be picking me up at the resort, so we together (you know, future husband and wife) could take Father Diego (you know, the priest who was going to be performing our wedding ceremony) to the airport. He texted me back so angry I would even question him.

Kiersten, I told a priest I would take him to the airport, I can't not do it.

Oh, *that* he can commit to.

And to be fair, I've been the third wheel smashed inside a car as a couple fights before—it's incredibly awkward, but we actually weren't fighting. It was just James going back and forth trying to decide if he actually loved me or not as I sat helpless like a wounded bird in the backseat.

Okay, yeah…that's super awkward.

Fine, Diego. You can have that one.

crushed

"This is all really heavy talk; I feel like it would be better over a beer. I have time before my flight," Diego offered. James's mood shifted instantly, and in all his terrible-driver glory, he cut off two cars, so we could about-face and end up at the Marriott hotel bar just outside of LAX.

James seemed utterly intrigued by the guy in the passenger seat, who was the literal opposite of everything he had been taught about religion. Not only did Father take a vow of chastity (and what says opposite of James more than that?), but he also took a vow of poverty.

No, not, like poverty...but *poverty.*

He was part of an order that serves the poorest of the poor, sitting knee-to-knee with souls most of our society has cast aside. I mean, the guy literally closed his bank account the day he took vows. So, when he offered to grab beer, James was like, "I'm buying," and Father was all, "Of course you are; I don't have a bank account."

Within minutes of us sitting down, the James I knew and loved was coming back to life, no longer angry and cold, but looking at me with such love as he recounted the last two years to Father. From our first meeting to James's reservations on marriage, to the fact he only knew one happily married couple, to his MO of keeping secrets, to what those secrets were. I could tell James was finding such ease chatting with someone so humble, someone who had literally heard it all and never once was surprised at James's experiences or feelings. I felt hopeful.

"I can tell you how much you want this to work."

James looked at me then and squeezed my hand; tears were coming to the surface for both of us.

35

kiersten lyons

We dropped Father off at the airport a few minutes later, with more than a few stares. Here was this pious man of God trying to not flash everyone in his robe as he got out of the low seats of the Audi convertible, with a tear-stained girl (that's me) thanking him profusely for everything because I was so sure he had fixed it all. That his suggestion of James and I not talking for the next week and instead using him as an objective sounding board for counsel was exactly the right medicine for what ailed our relationship. That his belief in us could help James to believe in himself. James got out of the car and shook Father's hand, so deeply touched for his listening, his wisdom, and his wise suggestion of grabbing a beer.

James and I drove home holding hands (except for the numerous moments James needed both hands on the wheel). I was scared, yes, because of his driving, but mostly because we'd come to these moments a few other times, where James would get scared, so sure he couldn't do it—and then the minute we were together again, he was sure, and he was ready.

"Baby, don't cry. It's okay—we'll see each other in a week. I love you. I want to marry you. We're going to get married." He held my face in his hands and kissed my damp cheeks. "I'm not going anywhere."

I turned to get out, but my eyes found the floorboards, and I was immediately taken back to a year and half before, curled up on them, so confused as the guy I loved told me it was over, told me it was all too much. I looked at him again, desperate for history not to repeat itself. "You're not going anywhere?"

"Not anywhere. I promise."

crushed

Our lips met gently, and then I climbed into my car and watched him drive away, begging God to not let go of him.

APRIL 2009

Right before my roommate moved back to Texas and I put all my stuff in storage to couch surf before the wedding, we had a movie night. We rented *Sex and the City*, which had just come to Redbox or some other such 2009 nonsense, and ate takeout, as was our usual Sunday night routine. And what a routine it was: we'd order from California Pizza Kitchen just across Sunset Boulevard and then pick it up, passing the IT nightclub—at the time it was Hyde, with all its paparazzi just waiting to grab a shot of Britney or Paris—and making our way back up to our apartment. More than once, I'd mess with them, pulling my hair over my eyes as we walked past. The flashes would go off until they realized...

"Never mind, she's nobody," they would call out to each other. That was me in LA, and oftentimes me with James. *She's nobody.*

Sex and the City held so much of my LA experience—and I know you're thinking, "Uh, it takes place in Manhattan, you dummy," but I actually watched my first landlord's entire VHS collection when I had just moved to LA. Lonely and in need of friends, those four women held everything that was grown-up and fancy. No longer was my mom around to tell me I couldn't watch it; I devoured the mature situations and pithy dialogue, not realizing how true to life it would be for me.

Well, you know. Except for the whole sex part.

Because as Carrie headed into the museum to wed a Big who didn't show up, I sardonically called out, "You know that's going to be me…."

My roommate whipped her head around, "Kiersten, that's not funny!"

I looked down at the Tiffany's solitaire on my finger, assuring her I was kidding.

THE LAST WEEK OF MAY 2009

The red leather booths of the steakhouse felt just as slick as the ones in the Audi, proving to everyone in the place that it was indeed luxury, yet it felt anything but.

A few days before, fresh from James assuring me he wasn't going anywhere, I went somewhere: Phoenix. Staying with my best friend Amy was already on my "pre-wedding couch surfing calendar" but the steak dinner she was now dragging me to in Phoenix was not. *Excuse me, Scottsdale*—and if you know anything about Scottsdale, it's dripping with people dying to be thought of as luxurious. But Amy wanted to take me to do something special, something that said: "If James is in Mexico, we're at least going to dinner!"

Oh yeah, during that week we were supposed to be using Father as a sounding board, really checking in with ourselves for clarity, James went to Mexico.

For his bachelor party.

I knew this because I checked in with Father Diego on Tuesday. Well, I called him at the friary (because that's the thing about taking a vow of poverty—you don't just not have a bank account, you don't have a cell phone either). So, like

crushed

it was 1994 again, I called up a landline, knowing a host of different people could answer as I nervously asked if Father Diego was there. Nervous because with every passing day, my fate was becoming clearer: James had yet to call him.

And so, on a Thursday evening, Amy took me out for a leather-booth-ed dinner, complete with an impromptu photo shoot.

My nose was red from crying, but I pretended to look happy so that when Amy posted it on Facebook, James would see it and realize how much he loved me (a gentle reminder, we're still in the year of our Lord 2009, thus Mark Zuckerberg is still very cool, Meta's not a thing, and no one knows we're being data mined). Amy did her best to make the night special, but it felt more like a last meal before the firing squad than your typical Scottsdale bachelorette party.

The next morning, I paced back and forth on the mattress I had been sleeping on. Amy and her roommate had an extra room, but with only a mattress on the ground they had lovingly made up.

What is up with me and mattresses on the floor during a breakup?

Only the mattress wasn't made up anymore; the sheet and blanket were scattered about, a testament to my lack of sleep the previous night.

My heart raced with every ring of the friary's phone. *Ugh, why can't the guy have a cell? I understand the whole vow of poverty and true humility and living among the poor and blah blah blah absolute genuine goodness, but I DON'T HAVE TIME FOR GENUINE GOODNESS, and why can't it just be easier to talk to this guy who held my fate in his hands as I am sinking into the depths of hell and*—"Oh, hello there—is Father Diego there?"

"Yes, let me find him. Who can I say is calling?"

Oh, you know, just the girl that's literally shaking in an oncoming panic attack because she's pretty sure Father is about to tell her that he still hasn't heard from her fiancé, is what I wanted to yell, but instead I softly said, "Kiersten."

I don't recommend having your heart cut out of your body in Phoenix on a Friday in late May. It's disgustingly hot, like a teen boy making a TikTok trying to fry an egg on his car's dashboard kind of disgustingly hot, but I had no choice, because like it or not I was here, and it was happening.

I wanted to walk, I needed to get out, to go, but it was 107 degrees, and a four-mile jaunt like the last time my heart was ripped out wasn't really an option. I blasted my car's AC, but it wasn't ready just yet, and hot air blasted my face.

Wasn't ready. That's what James had said in the email to Father. That he wasn't ready. He didn't know if he would ever be. He didn't want to marry me. He just needed to be on his own and figure his own stuff out.

Was all that hot air too?

Once again, I found myself in a large church. I didn't want to end up here—in fact I tried everything not to, because I'd already been to one church or another every day since coming to Phoenix, begging God to fix this, and right now it was truly the last place I wanted to be. But I couldn't go back to Amy's. I couldn't go anywhere in public because, well, I looked like someone who'd been punched in the

crushed

face with grief, and I definitely couldn't stay in my stupid non-luxurious car that was struggling in the 107-degree heat.

The church was silent. No one was there that day except the saints staring back at me. *I bet they have never felt heartbreak like this.*

Okay, yes, many of them had lost children, others spouses, many suffered horrible abuse at the hands of their oppressors, oftentimes enslaved, a lot had been murdered, but none of them had their wedding called off while the guy was at his bachelor party after he had cheated at the Magic Castle the night after he proposed and then probably a bunch of other times too!

What I'm saying is at no point was I thinking rationally. What I'm also saying is comparative suffering is never good; no matter what someone is going through, their grief, especially in the moments of the deepest pain, deserves to be honored, witnessed, and validated. But also, coming out of it, humor is possible, and laughter will return.

…But not at this moment.

I cried deep, silent tears, trying to hold the sound in, but what was the point? I was the only one there. Completely alone.

Oh, my God. I am completely alone.

The realization hit hard and fast, and now my shoulders shook almost violently. I could hardly catch my breath as the pain swirled throughout because it wasn't just the alone part, it was something else, something I couldn't quite put my finger on (and wouldn't realize for weeks) that left me somehow even more vulnerable, more exposed.

kiersten lyons

And then suddenly she appeared. Don't worry—I'm not going to try to convince you that an angel came or some apparition of Mother Mary, although, to be fair, I never saw this woman come in or go out, but suddenly she was there. Sitting right behind me as I tried to muster the strength to calm my shoulders and stop the tears (and snot) from pouring down my face. I was embarrassed but too weak; I couldn't stop the show of outward pain no matter how hard I tried. For five minutes she sat behind me, letting me know I wasn't alone, and then so gently and in the warmest voice, she began to pray in Spanish.

Ugh, why did I take French in high school?

It didn't matter, because within seconds my shoulders began to slow, my breath began to regulate, and even though I didn't understand any of it, I understood all of it. And then the most maternal, sweetest arms wrapped around me, and she told me I was loved. Over and over until I sort of believed it. There was pain in her own voice as she squeezed me so tight and told me to "just keep telling God my pain." I just knew she had sat in the same place as me, telling God her own pain over and over. I knew she knew grief.

She squeezed me one last time, telling me again how loved I was. And then she was gone. I wanted to turn around, to thank her, but I couldn't move. I just sat there grieving so deeply for the life I thought I was supposed to have yet wanting the peace she had offered me. And somehow, this time, I knew I would never have that peace with James.

And that, my friends, is called *clarity*.

crushed

It's so beautiful and will fill you up and make you think you can do anything…until it completely disappears. What I'm saying is this: **write that shit down.**

If, while you are reading, you find yourself having the gift of clarity about anything or anyone, *please* write it down: in your notes app, a scrap sheet of paper, or on this very page.

No, but seriously, you're going to need it—because at some point (give or take twenty-three minutes), you're going to pass a Rite Aid, and suddenly you're standing in the Rite Aid off Sunset where he started playing hide and seek that one time, and you both had laughed so hard that you almost peed your pants, and how could he forget? He would tell you all the time he'd never had as much fun with anyone as he had with you, and you know that he cheated, but he's never had a strong male role model, and if he would just—

JUNE 3, 2009

I hadn't updated my Facebook status since this whole thing started just two weeks before. But just because I hadn't updated my profile doesn't mean I wasn't constantly refreshing to see if he had.

I typed in my login on my parents' desktop, my hands still shaking from the phone call not five minutes before.

James and I had finally talked because he was finally back from his "boys' week." A term he coined because there was no longer a wedding, thus he was no longer a bachelor—although by ABC standards, any single man is one, but I let him have that because I was in no shape to fight. I must've missed a letter in the password because it wouldn't log me in.

kiersten lyons

How much else had I missed?

James's words swirled in my head as I typed the password in again, each sentence contradicting the previous one. He knew he loved me, but he didn't think he was *in* love with me. His friends didn't like that I was trying to change him (he apparently assured them it was his decision to investigate faith), but also his friends loved me. He needed to work on himself if we were ever going to work; he didn't want me to wait. I told him I would. He said no.

I told him then that I needed to not talk to him. I couldn't keep going back and forth. He said he understood, but I didn't want him to understand. I wanted him to say, "No. I can't live without you! I see it now!"

My Facebook profile appeared, like usual (except it wasn't usual) and any Facebook sleuth worth their salt would know the telltale sign: my status had gone from "Engaged to James" to "Engaged." Within seconds of getting off the call with me (or hell, maybe while we were talking) he deleted me as a friend.

He never even saw the one photo I was so sure would change everything.

crushed

But thank God he didn't (no, but *seriously*), because as much as those last two weeks in May held the deepest pain I had ever known, soon they would hold my greatest joy.

But if anyone would have told me that at that moment I would have punched them in the throat, because that is a cruel joke, and how dare you?!

Chapter Five

the list

JULY 2008

James and I had just gotten back from visiting New York together and having lunch with his dad when he asked if he could take my Little Sister, Ashley, and me out to celebrate three years of being matched through Big Brothers Big Sisters. Pixar's *Wall-E* had just been released, and James wanted to go to the famous El Capitan Theatre on Hollywood Boulevard to see it.

The Disney El Capitan Theatre is right off Hollywood and Highland, right next to Jimmy Kimmel's stage, across from Grauman's Chinese Theatre and its famous handprints, and just diagonally from the Dolby Theatre where they host the Oscars, and the

> Started in 1904 Big Brothers Big Sisters is the largest mentoring network matching volunteers to kids with "the belief that inherent in every child is incredible potential." In 2005 I began the process of applying to be a Big Sister, and by July of that year, Ashley and I were matched. She called me Kiki and I began to call her every week to hang out.

crushed

whole thing is surrounded by streets filled with the Hollywood Walk of Fame stars. What I'm saying is: it's the quintessential first thing anyone visiting LA wants to see (well, besides the restaurant from *Vanderpump Rules*). Also, what I'm saying is: these few square blocks were annoying to get to, crawling with tourists, and so expensive to park at, which made James asking to take Ashley and me there on a Friday even more touching.

Ashley and I had spent the last three years spending most Fridays (our day we'd hang out) grabbing fast food, window shopping, and maybe a cheap movie theater—I mean, I could barely afford the gas to pick her up in south LA, so movie theaters like Disney's El Capitan (and its adjoining ice cream parlor) were out of the question. But this was James we're talking about, and for the last four months, he'd been in full court press mode really trying to assure me he had changed.

Ashley liked James right away, and I honestly can't remember if they had met before this, but this moment, this late afternoon, with the large deluxe snacks in her tiny lap, James and I on either side, I will never forget. It was the moment I chose to trust him again. He was making her laugh, selflessly rushing out of the theater to grab more napkins and looking at me with all the boyish charm a boy could throw at a girl, and well…I was done for. Which made not even a year later even that much more crushing…

JUNE 2009

"Hi, Ashley, it's Kiki."

"You okay? You sound different."

kiersten lyons

"Yeah, um…"

If I thought I was shaking at the church…

"Ashley, James and I are not going to—"

I was so devastated to tell her. Her examples of men hadn't always been great, and this was just one more to add to the list.

"You and James aren't going to what?"

"James and I aren't getting married. He really is struggling and um…I'm just so sorry, I know how much you love him."

She paused, and then with all the wisdom of an eleven-year-old who's shouldered way too many burdens that were not hers to carry, "Kiki, I liked James, but I love you."

Aaaaand I lost it. I was trying my best to keep the tears silent, to make sure she knew it was okay for her to be the kid, and I would be the grown-up, but her words were too touching, too exactly what I needed to hear.

"Kiki, you okay?"

I assured her I would be (*did I just lie to a kid?*) and told her I was going to work at a camp in Maine for the summer. She told me she was going to the pool. We chatted about how boys can hurt our feelings sometimes, how James wasn't a bad guy but had just made some bad choices, and then she had to go. You know, to the pool.

I had emailed Monique at Maine Teen Camp a few days before I called Ashley, days before James finally called me himself to tell me not to wait for him. Even though I was now safe at my childhood home in Maryland (you know, sans the dehydrated bike ride), I knew I couldn't go back

crushed

to LA any time soon—the town where it seemed like every other car was a black Audi and every other girl was someone James had hooked up with.

Maine Teen Camp (or MTC) was and is an incredibly special place. I had been a counselor there the summer before I moved to LA, the summer I decided to leave college and pursue my dreams. I had been all of twenty while most of the counselors were in their mid-to-late twenties and Australian. Now in my late twenties (although still American), I figured this would be a great way to distract my broken heart.

I wanted to go pour into others, to have routine, to be around people who would know nothing of James or weddings or "not being pretty enough" for TV shows (besides, I was in no place to audition, and summers were slow anyway). But it was such a long shot—I mean, it was weeks before staff training, and did they even remember me?

I later found out a staff member had emailed the day before letting them know she couldn't make it that summer, and Mo (short for Monique) had thought they would be fine with the staff-to-teen numbers but woke up that morning realizing they needed to fill the position. Enter the email I had sent through tears the night before; it was the definition of perfect timing, and it wouldn't be the last time God would hold me close as James let me go. But at this moment, I refused to believe God had anything other than hurt to cause.

It had only been a week since running into two engagement sessions in one day, people—I was unwell.

I arrived at camp only to realize that they now staffed through a new company. No longer were my fellow coun-

kiersten lyons

selors late twenties, Australian, and tan, but early twenties, mostly British, and very pale.

"You're twenty-eight?! What kind of moisturizer do you use?"

No, but seriously—that is what a fellow counselor, all of nineteen years old (and American) asked me the day I arrived, as we, the new staff, sat in the lodge during a rainstorm getting to know each other. I was grateful for the rain; it gave me a chance to race back to my cabin to grab a jacket (and grab a quick cry).

I had spent much of past few days before that arrival day in my childhood bedroom in the basement screaming from the depths of my soul, mostly just the F word over and over—it was the only thing that brought some relief. But now I was in public and had to have a less "hot mess" and more "yeah, I can definitely be responsible for the safety and well-being of a bunch of teens for a whole summer" kind of vibe. Although apparently, according to that nineteen-year-old, I was looking great (you know, for a twenty-eight-year-old hag).

Monique and her husband Matt knew my deal and let me "grab a jacket" a few times through that week of training.

> And, please know, if you're ever a counselor at MTC and find yourself heartbroken, please reach out to me for all the best crying spots.

On our last night of training before the first round of kids arrived, we circled around the large fireplace in the expansive wooden lodge. Matt and Mo were sharing about what a gift this summer would be for each

crushed

of us, how the unique opportunity of getting to teach, support, and be a sounding board for these teens would change us, yes, but also how our relationships with each other would offer us change too. Matt and Mo had met as counselors at camp, and at this point, years later, were the directors (a few years after this summer they would become the owners, too). As Matt told the story of how they met, he looked over at Mo, his face illuminated by the campfire, and I was struck with his immense love and respect for her. He spoke about her with such tenderness, but also honesty and humor, how he'd never met anyone who was so fully themself.

So fully herself...

And that's when it hit me: the full realization of my shaking shoulders at church. Of exactly why not just my heart but my whole body ached.

For the first time in my whole life, I had been fully myself, and James had fully rejected me.

DECEMBER 12, 2008

"I promise. Every hour I'll call."

I shrugged, honestly not even knowing if I wanted him to.

James and I had just gotten into a fight about his driving. Well, mine actually, but really very much his too. Which I'm now realizing almost everything in our relationship was this—him projecting, me taking it as if it was always my fault, always something I needed to fix. Except this Friday was different.

I had been driving us on Highland, had just passed Hollywood Blvd and the El Capitan Theatre, when something

kiersten lyons

happened (maybe I switched lanes too quickly; I can't remember), and James gasped, startling me, which he had every right to—passenger driving in LA Friday traffic isn't for the faint of heart, and I had definitely made a mistake. Except that this is what I did to him often (because let's not forget he was a terrible driver, which led to lots of gasps from me, no matter how many times I tried to hold it in). Each time I got scared, each time I winced or jumped, he would scowl and then yell at me, angry I didn't trust him or his driving.

Yes, yes, I do see how poetic this all is.

The minute he gasped, I started crying, not soft, sad tears, but the angry ones, the ones filled with the exhaustion of almost a year and a half of walking around on eggshells because of him, of everything I was always doing wrong, and here he was *doing the exact same thing.* Something snapped, to which I said, "I don't know if I can do this anymore." He thought I meant driving, but I meant us.

It was a sweet and crisp gift of clarity (I didn't have this book yet to remind me to write it down, but you do now, so please do).

I told him how I am constantly doing everything I can to love him well and support him, and in the moments I am human, he gets so deeply angry that I would offend him, hurt his feelings, or not be completely smitten with him that he yells. I couldn't live like this anymore. As much as I wanted to love him like Christ (as we Christians love to say), I was not Christ. I was a human, and I had to be with someone who would let me be one.

crushed

"I don't even know if you love me," I said. "All you do is find fault with how I act, with who I am."

The clarity of it all!

As I was dropping him off, he promised to call me every hour to tell me one thing he loved about me. I nodded my head, but honestly, I was in no place to hear it. I was not just feeling this clarity but also *freedom* on top of that. At that moment, I didn't care if I said or did anything to make his little boy self have a temper tantrum; in that moment, I was done.

But he wasn't.

A bit later I received an email. One that was contrite. Dare I say *humble*? He suggested that we start over, even acknowledged how much he'd messed up, how much I gave and how much he took, and he said all of this with the understanding that he didn't even have a right to propose any of it. What I didn't know is that he was proposing all of this because two days later he would propose.

"Number twenty-seven: I love your freckles."

James was true to his word. Every hour on the hour since our fight in the car, James had called to tell me one thing he loved about me. Each one was detailed, sometimes covering childhood wounds I didn't even know were there. One was about my nose, the nose some in casting had told me to change, the nose I was always insecure about. I tried to hold close that short burst of clarity, that feeling of freedom, but

kiersten lyons

it was soon drenched in the sweetness he had been pouring for the last twenty-seven hours. It was so sweet that I began making a list.

Oh, that I decided to write down.

As much as I walked on eggshells during our relationship, I also somehow showed up completely myself. I didn't hide or pretend I was anything but me. I was funny and loud, I didn't shy away from my faith or my desire for greatness, I didn't shy away from my weirdness, I communicated what I needed and wanted, and I loved him with everything I had. He looked at all of that, at all of me, and two nights (forty-seven hours and details) later, he got down on one knee on the balcony of the Chateau Marmont to whisper the forty-eighth.

I wrote each down, forty-eight tiny details that not only proved his love, but (as I realized much later) proved I was, in fact, lovable.

I treasured that list for the next five months, tucked away in my nightstand, kept safe when all my stuff went into storage, until we ended up on another balcony with me throwing the ring at him.

My once treasured list crumbled as I clung to it through those two weeks of purgatory as he called the wedding off and on and then finally off again. What once had proven his love, what once had been so precious, now haunted me. It followed me to Maine like the worst camp ghost story, each detail resting in me as proof of my lack of worth, proving everything I always knew to be true: I didn't matter.

crushed

JULY 21, 2009

The campfire flames flickered and popped, but we were no longer in the lodge, no longer in beginning of camp. It was now mid-season, and some of my favorite campers were about to perform a song on their last night. They shifted nervously as I winked in their direction, then crossed my eyes and pulled in my chin to create seventeen more chins, hoping the silliness would distract them from their nerves. It worked; they all giggled. One nudged me and I almost toppled over, which made them laugh harder. I noticed my arms as I pulled myself up, now covered in freckles from the summer sun.

My freckles...

Two nights before I had called James. A lot.

One might say I blew up his phone. I wouldn't, but one might.

July 19. It was the date we were supposed to fly to New York for our wedding, and I was...having some feelings. He never picked up, and I woke up with a terrible hangover. Oh, not from alcohol—I had realized in college that alcohol can be a depressant for me (obviously I wasn't listening in high school health class) and knew if I had any shot at being okay through this whole grief thing, I couldn't drink. Like, at all. No, this hangover was of the vulnerability kind, because I didn't just blow up his phone with calls; I left voicemails.

A lot of voicemails.

I looked like death the morning after. Monique gave me a look during breakfast that was all, "Hey, I'm getting my mas-

kiersten lyons

ter's to be a school counselor and…you good?" I just looked the other way. Embarrassment doesn't even come close to a strong enough word for what I was feeling. So much shame. So, what did I do?

Wrote him an email, of course!

Please note right after he called off the wedding, I had emailed him then too—a goodbye, if you will. It was *pages*, and if I thought I was embarrassed after blowing up his phone, it is nothing to how I feel now reviewing these emails.*

*My research for this book has been thorough, none more exhaustive than combing through the emails I have saved from over that time— from sent to rambling drafts, they are filled with details and dates and so much pain. I saved them not for posterity, but for my little sisters, my possible future daughters for each one to know, in her own time of heartbreak, she can meet their sister or mom in real time of her own heartbreak and know she isn't alone. It has been gut wrenching to read through them, perhaps this one more than the rest. Not because of how cold it was, or how incredibly hurtful his lack of accountability felt, but that I allowed someone to treat me like this, over and over.

My walk of shame email the morning after was raw, because on one hand, it apologized for blowing up his phone, and on the other, it begged for clarity. How could he so casually throw out the person he loved like a piece of trash?! It was everything Taylor could want for a song, and I got back everything John Mayer could offer in a response.

crushed

James's response was long winded as he explained that he knew he'd never understand how hurt I'd been, but he had his "own share of shit to deal with," and before I got all defensive, he let me know he "was a part of this as well." He went on to say, "Come up with whatever well-thought-out conclusion you can, but I just never took it as seriously as you did." (*I'm sorry—you never took it as seriously? You were the one who proposed!*) Then he told me not to feel like a piece of trash just because he "realized it wasn't right."

Just because you realized it wasn't right?! YOU CHEATED ON ME THE NIGHT AFTER—

If I had ever questioned my acting ability, I needn't have, because here I was in a little area of the lodge, above dining, looking at an ancient computer screen as my whole life flashed before me, as the fifteen-year-old next to me typed out to their mom that they still hadn't received their sunscreen. I was so chill as I printed out James's email, like, *Oh this? Just a casual printout of an email that's definitely not written by a narcissist that I will pour over for the next three years.*

What I'm saying is your girl deserves an Academy Award for that performance. With a smile on my face (because sunscreen kid), I began a response. A response that took a week.

Because just like we need to write down the moments of clarity, we also must write down all the questions swirling in our head, to acknowledge all the pain that's longing to be seen. You must remind the guy who cheated on you, over and over, that you held his head in your lap. That you wiped away his tears as he said over and over what a horrible

kiersten lyons

person he was, how you don't even know how bad a guy he is. You have to get it out that it was you who deserved to be comforted as you cried, not him. You have to ask him why, after he called off your wedding, he had the audacity to tell your sister, "If I ever want to be a part of your family, I have to figure myself out." You have to ask him how the hell he could say that knowing it would give you hope when he had already realized such a simple thing like "it just wasn't right."

So here I was two days later, email still not finished (but don't worry, that kid's sunscreen had arrived). It was becoming a masterpiece of a letter, written in my journal, on the computer, and often in my head, as was the case when I sat at that campfire watching the flames pop and twist.

Number twenty-seven: I love your freckles. Were those forty-eight things just to get me to say yes? Some plot to make sure your proposal (because I'm now realizing it was never about me) that your proposal would—

I didn't have time to finish the thought because my campers' names were called, and just like that, they, the youngest ones there, were standing in front of the entire camp. Look, I don't know if you've ever been a teenager before (my gut says you have), but being freshly out of seventh grade and getting up in front of rising seniors in high school to sing a song is scary and brave—and did I mention scary? And yet here were these girls, my campers, looking straight at me taking a deep breath to sing. I made the silly face once more. They smiled and then sang their hearts out.

crushed

I don't remember the song. I don't remember if they were off key or on. I just remember their faces and how much they knew I deeply believed in them.

I never sent James those pages of the response I had poured over, because the more I wrote, the more I realized he'd never be able to actually receive it—another bit of clarity. So, I emailed it to myself and sent him this instead:

I surrender, I don't understand anything. I've got no defensives left. Because of your selfishness and lack of honesty, you have caused an overwhelming amount of damage and hurt, and I hope one day you can make amends to me.

I never heard back.

It would take me years to fully believe I mattered and that his engagement list didn't, but on that night, with my campers singing their hearts out as the fire roared, I began to. Because as heartbroken I was, as defenseless as I felt, I was reminded of something I had lost sight of, I still had something to offer...

And I promise, without a shadow of a doubt, that you do too.

Because that's the gift of heartbreak. And I know you may want to push me down a ravine right now for calling any of what you're feeling a gift, but it is. Because once you've sat in the pain of rejection, the cruelty of abandonment, or the exhaustion of hopelessness, once you've known the depth of having no more defensives, then you can see it in another light.

kiersten lyons

And I promise you, there is nothing more beautiful than seeing someone else, nothing more worthy than sitting next to them to remind them of their worth, because it is in seeing them that we just might see ourselves.

Chapter Six ♡

oh sh*t, it's real

SEPTEMBER 2009

I spent the most heartbreaking summer at a little camp in Maine. I also spent the most magical summer at a little camp in Maine, but it was time for reality—it was time to go back to LA. And so, on September 10, 2009, I boarded a plane from Nashville (more on that later) and went home.

And, yes, it was literally a month after Miley's "Party in the USA" arrived to radio, and so, of course, I listened to it as the plane touched down at LAX, and no, I am not offended if you want to pause reading this to listen to it right now. It's a masterpiece on every level.

Also, I do realize the irony of typing the words *reality* and *Los Angeles* in the same sentence unless one is referencing a Bravo show, but alas, my reality was LA, and nothing was reminding me of it more than James's freaking Olive Garden commercial!

Because that shit was playing *a lot*, which was truly annoying on two accounts: one, his face was in my face often,

kiersten lyons

but two (and maybe even worse), it meant that trust fund boy was getting residuals. You know, money, lettuce, cheddar...

Probably unlimited breadsticks too!

And so, I did what anyone healing would do: I called him.

Look, we all know there are five stages of grief—some people go through them all, and some don't. They aren't linear, and there's no true order. All this is science-based, evidence-based, fact-based, blah blah blah Brené Brown. And I had hit them all (and then some) in the last almost four months. I was good—I mean, did you not see that email response?

"I surrender...."

Hello—that's acceptance, which is the last one! I just called him for business stuff, like, "Do you remember the name of the storage facility where my stuff is, because you have the documents, oh and why don't I come over and we'll have sex?"

Yes, yes, I did offer my body, which I'm sure is especially confusing to you as that was a whole thing in our relationship, right? Which is why I was offering, duh! It's really simple: we sleep together, he realizes what he missed out on, we get back together, and it's happily ever after! I really don't see how this is that hard for you to understand...

No, Cheryl, I'm not squarely in the anger phase with a side of bargaining wrapped up in denial!

WHY WOULD YOU EVEN ASK ME THAT?!

There was a pause, then "I don't think that's a good idea." Then I was all, "I do."

crushed

If my memory serves me right, I believe the call ended with me crying out, "Why did you call me my first name and middle name with your last name attached if you never planned on marrying me?!"

My heart was racing, and I honestly don't remember if one of us hung up on the other, but I remember staring at the phone, at his number.

That fucking number.

I hated that thing. He was so proud to have an old school 917 Manhattan number and would talk about how it meant he was a real New Yorker. So real, one time his roommate (you know the one who didn't think I was hot enough) said we should all go to Barney's, and James got so excited, saying, "I have a credit card there!"

We all gave him a weird look. "You have a credit card to the local bar Barney's Beanery?"

"Oh, I thought you meant Barney's New York...."

You know the insanely expensive store to grab up-and-coming designers like Chanel and Prada? This is what the guy I wanted to spend the rest of my life with deemed authentic, real, genuine—the fact he had that area code and a credit card to that store? Why did I love this guy so much? Why did I want him back? Why was my thumb reaching out to call him again?!

In panicked desperation, I threw the phone across my room. Sike, not my room—because remember? I am currently without housing, and let's not forget the apartment search, which led to a potential roommate who worked with James, and when I said, "Well, now you know why I'm looking for

63

a place." And she looked at me confused, and I go, "Because he called off the wedding," and she goes, "Huh, I didn't even know he was engaged."

No, I was staying with my friend Sage again, and while she was currently out at an acting class, her roommate had very much just come home, so I did what any girl would do: grabbed a pillow to squash all sound and wept bitterly into it.

"You counted Steve twice!"

"No, I didn't! Look: one, two, three, four, five, and then *six* was JTT, so he gets crossed out. You're marrying Steve Urkel!"

My best friend Lauren and I were in the middle of a gripping game of recess MASH, and this round was not it. So far, I was going to marry Steve Urkel, live in a shack, and have seventy-nine kids, but my future could be redeemed. Okay, fine—personally, things weren't looking good, but professionally? Professionally, I still had something to hang my hat on. I still could become a famous actress and—

"—And six! You're going to be a trash man!"

Trash man was the absolute worst job (this was before we all grew up and realized sanitation workers make a great salary with solid benefits and weekends off), but at this moment, for a fifth grader in Germantown, Maryland, *trash man* was threat level midnight only confirmed by my yelping, "Noooo!" as Lauren's number-two pencil unceremoniously scratched out "famous actress." My wailing signaled to the rest of fifth grade to make their way over.

crushed

"Oh, Kiersten, I'm so sorry. I know how much you love to act." That was a girl from my Girl Scout troop. Her empathy was appreciated.

"Even Steve Urkel wouldn't marry you." That was from a stupid boy.

"Oh, honey, Jaleel White is very handsome." That was from the recess aide who was trying to make things better, but there was nothing she could do. My fate was sealed, and it was that of a dumpster fire.

Who knew fifth-grade recess could be prophetic…

I was so sure James would come back, so sure even though he said we weren't right, he would one day realize he was wrong.

I had fantasies of him showing up at camp breakfast, where announcements were made and previews of the night's activities performed. It wouldn't be extravagant, not like a counselor repelling down the walls of the lodge to preview a ropes night or even a bunch of us dressed like we were straight out of *Grease* to showcase a Sock Hop. No, it was going to be subtle, like as the bell rang for classes and the kids loaded up their dirty breakfast dishes, he would be standing there, just off from the grand staircase. His eyes would look up, boyish charm and all, as he told me how much he missed me, how there wasn't anyone like me, how he couldn't live without me.

But he *could* live without me. *Thrive*, apparently (oh, just wait), while I was still barely breathing.

kiersten lyons

No, but literally.

Because the pillow I had been smothering my face with (a la Othello) wasn't offering any air (also a la Othello). I pondered the relief for a second too long and then yanked it off me, scared I was enjoying the lack of air just a bit too much. It wasn't the first time things had gotten dark. I'd had despairing, dark thoughts a few times in my life, always surrounding a surge of pain wrapped in hopelessness, but this was different. This was it, the finale scratch of his name on the wide-ruled paper in the game of MASH that was my life.

I didn't have my dream job, my dream husband, my dream number of kids… I wasn't even living in a shack. I was sleeping on the other side of Sage's bed!

Look, here's the thing: I could tell you it was all my idea, that just after I called James begging, I had clarity again, knowing how much I needed help.

But that would be a lie. A BOLD-FACED ONE.

I met Katherine through James. They had worked together at Bar Marmont, and to say Katherine was beautiful would be an understatement. She was stunning, like, had a contract with Ford Models when she was still a young teen (or maybe it was Wilhelmina—I don't know. The point is girlfriend's face was the face all the casting directors wanted me to have). James told me the first night he met her he was immediately taken with her, and even when he found out she was married, he thought, "Well, how married?"

crushed

I ALMOST SPENT THE REST OF MY LIFE WITH THIS GUY!

Katherine wasn't just beautiful, she was also so incredibly kind, thoughtful, and loved God. Well, *now* she did, but not always. She told James upon meeting me, "I don't think you can do this. I'm not sure you understand how hard it is to be in love with someone who loves God, not to mention the whole no-sex thing. For her sake, let this girl go." (Or something to that effect....)

Apparently, my fifth-grade MASH wasn't the only thing prophetic.

Katherine knew—she had met her husband years before, and her husband loved God, and she thought that was cute but also weird, and both James and I were completely inspired by their story and reached out for thoughts often.

No, but like, *often*, often.

During both our breakups I leaned on Katherine (read: clung). It was odd for me; I was so used to being the big sister, the voice of reason, and here I was sobbing into the takeout Thai food she had just bought me the day after our first breakup, profusely apologizing. "I'm so sorry, I'm usually the one taking care of people. I swear I'm not usually like this."

I called her often, trying to understand James's point of view, but, if we're being honest, really trying to hold on to the hope that we would come back together, just like Katherine and Lukas did. But now there was no more holding, no more clinging; I had nothing left to offer after I had offered all of me and been so purely rejected.

kiersten lyons

"It's over. Really over."

It wasn't the first time I had told her this, but it was the first time I believed it.

"I think you should come to Al-Anon with me."

The meeting was in a building's basement of some sort; I don't remember. I just remember feeling so small, so helpless, and that wasn't just because there were celebrities among us.

And no, I won't tell you who they were—anonymous is literally in the name, so stop asking, Cheryl!

No, it was because I was facing the truth. If I was doing this, if I was walking into this meeting, if I was sitting down, it really and truly meant James wasn't the one (I know I've said it already—multiple times—but remember, grief is never linear, and acceptance can appear one moment and disappear the next).

One by one, hands went up to share, and that basement became all at once sacred and equally uncomfortable. Because telling the truth on ourselves can feel scary, but it's the only thing that leads to healing, to peace. The same peace I had known as the woman wrapped her arms around me so many months before returned. Her words echoed in my head: "Just keep telling God your pain."

I closed my eyes, listening to others share theirs: some removed by decades, and others that happened on the drive over, yet all being witnessed, all being seen. I was struck with their faces and the relief of telling the truth, the nodding heads, each of us feeling as if we were looking in a mirror. It wasn't that our details were the same; it was our longings, our aches, our ridiculously embarrassing moments that made

crushed

the room shake with laughter. All at once we weren't embarrassed, because all at once we were safe.

I stared down at the little notebook I brought, thinking I would get some burst of wisdom, some gift of clarity—I was finally ready to write it down, and—

This was the clarity!

Because before I couldn't...I wouldn't. If I dared to write any bits down, then that would mean they would be true, and I couldn't let clarity be true because I needed James. I needed us to be true.

Oh, shit...

I raised my hand, shaking the entire time. I don't remember what I said, but I remember the faces, the soft smiles, the nodding heads, and the hearty laughs when they understood what I was saying all too well.

The laughter was contagious, the peace overwhelming, and I was beginning to believe in the power of not only knowing you aren't alone, but the gift of sharing in another's heartbreak. That there is always someone beside you, whether you realize it or not, and another just in front and maybe one that's just behind, just starting out, but we'll never know that unless we tell the truth. I needed each of those stories to have the courage to sit in my own. I needed each of these stories to know I was going to be okay.

I needed each of these stories to have the confidence to tell you you're going to be okay.

When I was twenty-eight, I thought my whole world was ending—and for just a moment, it was. But as I watched a man share about his darkest moment a decade before, as I

kiersten lyons

watched his eyes fill with tears and then suddenly light up with laughter, I, for the first time, had hope that maybe my world wasn't ending, that maybe it was just beginning. That maybe the heartbreak was really just a symptom of the bigger issue, but to get there, we must go back to where it all began.

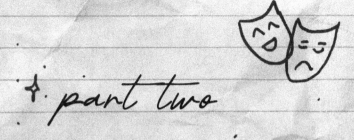

part two

"THE HOW DID I GET HERE?"

CUE: "MEAN" BY TAYLOR SWIFT

Before we get started, you have a task—a bit of a game, if you will. Well, you won't actually get to play said game until later in the book, but like anything good in life, it takes time to reach maturity (see: rude!)—but just go with me on this.

Your first name:_____

Your favorite color when you were a kid:_____

Your favorite stuffed animal:_____

Wonderful. Gold stars all around.

Chapter Seven ♡

i love you. i know.

My first love played with my older brother every afternoon.

Wait. Before I go any further, I should probably introduce my big brother, Luke. He was almost four years older than me, good at every sport, and so cool. I mean, he could talk like a Transformer.

I feel like you're not taking this seriously—my brother could talk like a Transformer. THEY ARE ROBOTS IN DISGUISE!

Also (and just a side note, I'm not even sure why I'm sharing it as it's probably not even relevant, but) Luke wanted nothing to do with me—like minutes after I was born asked my parents when I was going back to where I came from and told me repeatedly at any chance he could what a loser I was. Which is weird because I was like, super cooperative, and he was like, super not, so obviously he could have learned a thing or two from me, but whatever, it's cool because he was cool, and I'm sure that's the last we'll talk about him....

kiersten lyons

Anyway, back to my first love: He was handsome with a little crooked smile, and a gun belt.

His name was Han Solo, and for my fourth birthday, I desperately wanted my very own action figure, but when the presents were all opened, it was Princess Leia sitting there (stupid side buns and all). Her plastic white dress molded to her body just screamed, "Ooh I've totally got a metal bikini on underneath this."

I sat amongst my presents holding this trollop pretending to be a princess when my older brother (in a stroke of kindness not seen again that decade) threw an old Han at me.

"Here, I've got a bunch of him."

Once I stopped crying from the thing hitting me square across the cheek (I'm sure Luke didn't mean to throw it that hard, right?), I then began crying from how beautiful Han really was. I mean, sure his crooked smile was a bit faded, and his gun belt was turning an off shade of green, but those pants tucked into boots were still working.

Every afternoon, Han, Leia, and myself would play together in my backyard, but many days Princess Leia would have official business to attend to. I mean, hello, who else but a princess could knight all three of my Care Bears? Plus, princesses are Anglican, so of course she wouldn't be seen going to Mass with me. What would her subjects say? Oh, but don't worry, Han was Catholic, so he would be attending.

Our love was a secret, dangerous one…. Until one day when I heard a loud, grumbling sound, reminiscent of a lawn mower coming from the backya—

"HAN!"

crushed

I had left my beloved out the night before! I ran over to see Princess Leia with no head.

insert evil laugh

No. No. Stop. Kiersten, you are the cooperative one, the one with the good heart. There is no time for Taylor Swift–level revenge, only compassion. I need to find Han; surely, he escaped to save himself for me!

But before I could find my beloved, my brother came from the side yard, holding a twisted and lifeless Han.

"Look at what you did to my Han! Why are you such a loser?"

Before I could protest that it was the lawn mower, Han was being chucked at my head. Once I stopped crying from the pain of having a plastic figurine thrown at me (again), I began crying from the heartbreak; Han hadn't hidden himself away for me. He chose to perish with his precious Leia.

Han may have gotten mangled, but I got crushed.

But honestly, this did not compute. I mean, my parents told me roughly fifty times a day how spectacular I was, and spectacular people are very lovable!

kiersten lyons

My dad is somewhere between Alec Baldwin (you know, without all the yelling at service workers and gun stuff) and Santa Claus. He's the best storyteller (although you're never quite sure what percentage of the story is true). To him, his five kids are quite possibly the smartest, funniest, most incredible people to ever walk the face of the earth.

My mom is a bit more realistic—she was a parent educator (that's right, my mom taught other moms how to parent). I guess I can't really talk about her in therapy…just kidding, I talk about her all the time. And don't worry, she knows. The first time I told her I was going, she was all, "Great, talk about me!"

My parents were big believers in a strong self-confidence, which meant tons of praise (I'm the generation of participa-

crushed

tion trophies—you get it!). Thus, I believed that with every movement I made, I should be told I'm doing a great job.

"Kiersten, the way you packed your lunch shows creativity."

"Kiersten, I cannot get over how detailed this book report on *Sarah, Plain and Tall* is."

"Kiersten, I can really tell you've been practicing your round off."

I'd done that round off multiple times for Han, and still he chose Leia! *HOW COULD HE?!* I would shut myself in the kids' bathroom for hours asking myself this question. Literally asking myself in the mirror. You see, the bathroom was my absolute favorite place—for one reason: the mirror.

I could pull the mirrored medicine cabinet door just to the right to make three, four, or ten copies of myself. Soon I would forget about Han's rejection and entertain myself for hours, only to be interrupted each morning by my first introduction into relationship banter.

"Honey?"

"What?"

"It happened again."

"What?"

"I woke up even more handsome then yesterday. I'm sorry, but there will be a lot of ladies checking me out today!"

I needed to find my own best friend to yell narcissistic things to!

But I was five and starting to see that at twenty-nine years old, perhaps Han was a bit too mature for me. Still, the thrill of an older man led me straight to my next crush.

Chapter Eight

criss-cross applesauce

I think it's safe to say Han was my first criminal, but not my last.

Everyone marveled at the ease with which I taught my Cabbage Patch doll. My patience when she wasn't coming to circle time was a sight to behold. True, I learned many of these tools from my own mentors (i.e., my mom), but I also was just a natural and knew I was destined for a future in education.

I was a mature five and three quarters.

Kindergarten was a delight. I had my future all worked out—teachers' college, of course, and then making the boy with the 3-D robot on his sweatshirt my husband. The beads inside the clear tummy of the robot would pop up and down when he walked, so obviously he was a great choice for a life partner.

That is, until I met Kevin.

Well, I had already met him—he lived at the top of my street, played wiffle ball with my older brother in the

crushed

cul-de-sac every afternoon, and his dad was the only dad in the neighborhood who smoked cigarettes—but this was the moment I met his soul.

The buzz outside the multipurpose room was palpable as my class waited for our turn to file in. We watched bigger kids go first knowing they'd be seated behind us. My eyes studied the show poster scotch taped to the cinderblock hallway.

I couldn't read just yet (besides a good "Pat Sat on the Mat" tale), but my context clues told me this was all very exciting. Just then it was our turn to enter the hallowed cafeteria that boasted a wooden stage. It was my first time inside; kindergartners were half-day students and didn't have the pleasure of enjoying their lunch at this fancy establishment.

I'm sorry—wait one second. Does the stage have velvet curtains?!

I sat criss-cross applesauce on the cold linoleum floor just as the music began and my life as I knew it changed forever.

It was my first time seeing live theater, because a puppet show at the library does not count! Within minutes, Kevin appeared onstage, but instead of wiffle ball apparel, he was wearing a pleather jacket and a stippled-on beard.

He is so cool.

His character yelled at the orphans so loudly I had to cover my ears, but for some reason I had no desire to cover my eyes. As scary and vicious as he was, everything in me wanted to keep my eyes on him, even and *especially* as he pulled out a knife. The blade glistened in the multi-purpose room fluorescent lights.

kiersten lyons

He was so dangerous. Then all at once he lunged at Nancy, chasing her behind that fancy velvet curtain where she let out a scream. Minutes later he died too.

He was so dramatic....

They both peeked their heads out to let us younger ones know they were, in fact, okay, but it didn't matter. The damage was done. I loved the bad boy.

That afternoon, I tried to take my requisite nap, but all I could think about was Kevin and that beard.

The doorbell rang.

It was Kevin, looking for my brother.

"He's not here right now. Soccer practice."

He turned to go, and I took my chance.

"I really liked you in the school play. Especially the dying scene."

He turned and smiled, "What dying scene?"

Then he dropped to the ground, rolled, and died right there. *Just for me.*

"You know, I can't really die unless I have a Nancy."

"I can be your Nancy! You can even stab me a knife!"

"It's not a real knife. You touch it, and the plastic blade goes down. See?"

We spent the next few hours dying all over our neighborhood. Sometimes he would chase me to the mailbox, and I would die right there. And then we'd switch, and I'd run after him until I caught him. He died on our neighbor's lawn, and even twice in the middle of the street.

I was sure we'd do it all again the next day, on our second date, but what would I wear? I finally decided on my Daisy

crushed

Girl Scout uniform—that way he'd know I had pledged to take care of America. My mom said it was never good for a girl to wait by the phone, so I waited by the front door. The doorbell rang. I played it cool, smoothing down my uniform.

"Kevin, what a lovely surprise."

"Hey, is your brother home?"

I assumed he was playing hard to get, but just then my brother ran through the doorway, pushing me down. But Kevin didn't help me up. And that's when I heard the giggles...two giggling girls on the porch. *My* porch!

"Little sisters are the worst! Come on, let's go chase down the ice cream truck!"

And then the four of them ran up the street. No look back from Kevin. No acknowledgement of our beautiful afternoon together.

I mean, who dies with someone over and over again and then pretends like it didn't even happen?!

I knew what I had to do.

I walked into my room to let my dolls know the news: I was leaving teaching. I saw how Kevin held Nancy's hand at the curtain call; the theater was my home now.

It didn't take long, as that fall it was announced my first-grade class would be putting on the award-winning show *The Little Rabbit Who Wanted Red Wings.* My pivot to the performing arts wasn't completely out of the blue, as I put on performances in my driveway quite often to the stylings of "Splish-splash, I was taking a bath." Live theater was just the logical next step for me (and my relationship with Kevin).

83

kiersten lyons

We had auditions, and I gave it my all, truly putting myself out there. I was sure I would obtain the role I needed to prove to Kevin I was his match: The Little Rabbit. Plus, it was triple cast, so really not that hard, but just in case, I offered some prayers to God, letting him know how deeply I wanted the role, how cooperative I was, with the reminder that it was incredibly important for my future—marriage and career and all that jazz.

During reading groups (I was in the green reading group, thankyouverymuch), the cast list was posted. I scanned the top but didn't see my name. My eyes moved down the page, and each line seemed to bring Kevin into less focus, until I saw it: Miss Puddle-Duck.

Who the eff is Miss Puddle-Duck?!

Okay, fine, I get it. The entertainment business is rough; I gotta pay my dues. But I also need to show Kevin that I'm a woman about town. A woman who can go to the ice cream man alone. It's time to grow up.

I snuck into my parents' room because that's where they kept all the "Let's Talk" books. You know, the age-appropriate book to talk to your kids about tough stuff like drugs and sex and shoplifting. I found my favorite one; it was a cartoon book called, *Where Did I Come From?*

"Kiersten?"

"Yes, Mom?"

"I know some of your friends call it their flower or hoo hah, but we're going to call it by its real name. It's nothing to be ashamed of—it's just another part of your body. Like your elbow…. Vagina."

crushed

Which is why when I was three and got a doll whose batteries went in her crotch, naturally I called her my vagina doll. What I'm saying is your girl read that book cover to cover, trying to remember everything my mom had said.

"Kiersten, millions of sperm try to take that egg on a date, but just one very persistent sperm gets to marry that egg."

And yes, if you're wondering, that page's cartoon was a sperm with a top hat holding a rose. Naturally...

Okay, so to be grown-up, I need to be persistent. I'll show Kevin and Han Solo and that freaking cast list. No more "nos" for me; it's time for a yes!

In first grade, my little brother was born. He was super cute, and I was super excited to hold a baby (i.e., dress him in my old baby clothes I used for my doll. I would like to take this opportunity to apologize to you, Jack. You did not deserve that, but you also looked super cute). I also met my best friend, Lauren. She had everything I ever wanted (read: long hair). And you know who loves long hair? First-grade boys. Four days into recess, Lauren had a boyfriend, Jake. And Jake had a best friend, Matty. Matty had blond hair and freckles and was good at sports.

Huh, you know what's funny? My brother has blond hair and freckles and is good at sports. That's so random and probably means absolutely nothing....

Anyway—through my morning bathroom vent listening, I learned that relationships were more than just banter; they were about being interested in your partner's interests.

"Barry, how did your conference call go?"

85

kiersten lyons

"MaryPat, how long did it take to Spray 'n Wash that spaghetti stain?"

I brought my findings into the field. No, but literally, in first grade you got to have recess on the field.

"Matty, I like your New York Giants jersey."

"Which New York Giants is the best ball thrower?"

"Matty...what is a New York Giant?"

I was running out of New York Giant–themed questions one recess when Jake announced we'd be playing a new game called rugby. We would break into two teams and run around pushing each other over. Pretty soon we were tackling each other. Pretty soon Matty tackled me.

This is the greatest game ever invented.

I was sure that by showing him my brute strength it would make him like me more. He'd be all, "Wow, Kiersten, you're so strong. I wish I was Mr. Puddle-Duck, so we could be married."

Matty had been cast as Mr. Snake, and obviously I looked into offing Mrs. Snake, but she had been held back in kindergarten and could definitely take me (a New York Giant if you will...), so I stuck to tackling my man over and over, until one day I landed directly on top of him.

"Eww, Matty, it looks like your girlfriend's stronger than you!"

"Kiersten's not my girlfriend. She doesn't even like me."

I was still on top of him, not sure what to do next as his eyes pleaded with me to tell everyone I didn't like him. My face turned red, not sure what to do or say, as he pushed me off him.

crushed

"Well, I don't like her!"

The other boys laughed at me as Lauren wisely tugged my shocked self away.

This makes no sense! He answered every one of my New York Giants questions!

I went home that night looking for answers and found them in a one Mr. Alex P. Keaton. (You know, Michael J. Fox: short, witty, incredibly adorable, and a massive box office draw—the OG Jonathan Taylor Thomas.) He didn't like a girl until he realized he was being mean to her because he did like her!

My dad laughed. "Kiersten, boys that are mean to you will probably grow up to have a crush on you."

Ohhhhhh! Matty doesn't realize he loves me yet! I'll just have to show him. And maybe he'll be thickheaded like Alex. I'll have to be...what's the word my mom used...PERSISTENT!

Like the sperm in the top hat!

Chapter Nine

he's mean because he likes you!

Now I know what you're thinking. "What new information! I've never heard this before—what a gift that you are sharing this hard-won wisdom with us that is definitely true and not at all kind of toxic. You're the ultimate girl's girl: making sure to not gatekeep this relationship advice but sharing it with the world...."

It was such wisdom that I would base my entire personality around it for the next twenty years or so, not to mention the rest of that year...because I kissed Matty seven times in first grade.

Usually, I would run up behind him, put my hands over his eyes, and whisper, "Guess who?" and then I would kiss him on the cheek. He started to figure out my MO and did his best to stay clear of me, so I had to become a love spy and dangerously follow him until his back was to me.

The last time, I appeared from behind a tree and slapped my hands over his eyes, but he wiggled out of my embrace,

crushed

and what with me desperately trying to be affectionate, and him desperately trying to run away, our lips touched, and that's when he yelled, "I don't like you! You're ugly. Leave me alone."

Why would he say something so cruel to the woman he loves? Did he still not understand his feelings for me? I had to do some serious thinking. Once I got home, I made a beeline for the bathroom, my favorite place to ponder life (but also because I had to pee). I was on the toilet when I heard my brother, Luke, coming up the stairs. I didn't think anything of it until the door swung wide open. I tried to scoot over so the sink would cover me just as a parade of neighborhood boys walked by.

"Hey guys, look, it's my ugly little sister peeing!"

Ugly?

He immediately got grounded, and I immediately got offered ice cream as my dad told me I was beautiful over and over. Wait, was I ugly, or was I beautiful? Was the bathroom the best place in the world or the worst? Why am I going to completely skip my second-grade crush and move on to third? Because, clearly, I don't have all the answers, people. We're learning as we go!

Plus, second grade was a bit of a wash, not much to report—just that my mom had surprise twins. Yep, by the time I was in third grade, my parents had five kids (with the last two coming together even though the doctor and everyone else said there was only one). But they were girls! I had sisters, and within two minutes my dad started telling everyone that I prayed too hard for a sister and so out came two. This honestly made complete sense to me. *Hellooo*, I was so cooperative, obviously God was like, "I see you; I see you doing everything right—of course I have to give you what you want." Because that's definitely how prayer works!

But why didn't he hear me about Matty?

I didn't have time to ponder this existential question because third grade also saw my mom's first psychotic break. The combination of having three littles under three and her complete lack of sleep postpartum triggered it one morning when I woke up to find my mom in my room unaware of where she was. Immediately I had to step in and explain, confused that my mom was confused.

I was only eight and half, and within minutes of waking me up, she was telling me I couldn't trust my dad, and my dad was telling me now wasn't the time to listen to my mom, so I took it upon myself to not trust anyone. For a third grader who was already struggling to feel safe, this piled on a whole new layer.

It was now my job to take care of my three younger siblings, no matter if that role was actually given to me or not (it was a bit of both). And if you're wondering, yes, I did do it splendidly, and it surely didn't affect my views on love and completely sacrificing oneself for someone else. Surely this moment in time wouldn't become a core part of my identity that to feel worthy was to feel needed....

Besides, I had a new love, his name was Ryan, and he also had blond hair and freckles and was good at sports.

Huh…

crushed

Ryan and I were desk buddies, which meant our desks were pushed together, with one other student named Mike. Mike was only in our class for part of the day, as he was part of an inclusion program. He spent his mornings in a different classroom that provided additional support before joining us in the afternoons. It was incredible to have half the day alone in our own desk paradise, but it was even better when Mike came to hang out, because Ryan was so kind to him. And I don't think there is anything hotter than watching the boy you like teach someone else how to spread the glue on their hand, wait for it to dry, and then slowly pull it off. The three of us laughed so hard as we peeled the hardened glue off our raisin-y hands.

Ryan was going to make an amazing father, and I had to tell him how great he truly was.

"Mom, how do you spell admirer?"

"Did you look it up in the kid dictionary?"

My mom had been home from the hospital for quite some time and back to her old shenanigans, like helping us become independent and do things for ourselves, like making us look up our own words.

This letter needed some pizzazz, something to make it stand out. Long before telling Jonathan Taylor Thomas I liked gouda, I did something far more sinister than lie... I stole.

Bart Simpson was the coolest thing ever. I was not allowed to watch *The Simpsons*, which made stealing the picture my brother, Luke, had drawn of Bart to include in my letter even more thrilling. The rush of dangerous love choices

kiersten lyons

was becoming such a high. The next day I placed the envelope in Ryan's cubby.

Dear Ryan,

Bart Simpson is my idol and so are you. I think you're going to make a really great dad someday.

Love,
Your Secret Admirer

Well, of course I wasn't going to sign my name! I had to play it cool. Do you think I learned nothing from the Matty affair?!

Right before the greatest teacher in all the land, Mrs. Lennon, sat down for story time, Ryan grabbed the note. (Seriously, Mrs. Lennon was so amazing—when my mom was in the psychiatric hospital, I got to have a sleepover at her house. She even took me to the grocery store and let me pick out the Jolly Ranchers for our class jar, and she took me to see *All Dogs Go to Heaven*—a bizarre film she fell asleep in, but still—greatest teacher of all time!)

Okay, good—you read the letter, now look at me!

I tried so hard to listen to *Mr. Popper's Penguins*, but Ryan was now motioning over John to look at it.

No, not John!

In kindergarten John had been my best friend when he saved my Pound Puppy (the coolest stuffed dogs around) from drowning, but by first grade he began to ignore me,

crushed

and by third he was my archrival. And now he was turning around asking girls who their secret admirer was. Story time was over and I was doing my best to get Mike interested in putting glue on our hands again, but then John got right in my face.

"Who's your idol?"

The Elmer's glue must've been seeping into my bloodstream, because I got scared and blurted out, "Bart Simpson, I mean…the sister, Lisa, right? Is she the one who—"

But it was too late—John was already yelling back to Ryan, "Ewww Ryan, it's Kiersten! The girl who looks like a boy wants to have babies with you!"

But don't worry about me. By fourth grade everything made sense because I had a boyfriend!

It happened on the last day of fourth grade. All year I had asked Terrence out, and all year he had said no. (Well, technically not always no. One time I wrote him a note asking if he'd go out with me, and to check yes, no, or maybe; he didn't even check no—he just threw it away.)

But on the last day Lauren called him and then suddenly threw the phone to me, and I was all, "Hey, uh do you want to go out with me?" And he was all, "Fine!" And I was all, "I'm in a relationship!"

It was an intense summer; we saw each other once at the pool and each ignored the other, as all couples do. I mean, we were basically a Netflix romcom.

kiersten lyons

Fifth grade was going to be awesome; I had my first boy teacher, our classroom was in the portables (those were big time; they weren't even connected to the school!), and I began carrying a purse (which I promptly left in said portable that first lunch).

My Girl Scout friends and I were all at lunch, discussing our new venture capital friendship bracelets that were going to start selling at recess (ten cents a bracelet, but if you bought more than one, the price went to nine cents) and how dreamy our new boy teacher was when he approached. Not the teacher, not even Terrence—John!

What does this guy want?

"Terrence forgot he was going out with you this summer, so you're dumped."

The cafeteria hushed as I took a breath, and then with all the confidence of a girl who had just read an Ida B. Wells biography for summer reading, I exclaimed, "Well, if Terrence doesn't have the guts to say it my face, then we're still going out!"

All my friends cheered (because feminism) when I felt a tap on my shoulder.

Apparently, John wants some more. Well, guess what buddy, I read a biography on Susan B. Anthony too!

But it wasn't John.

"I forgot I was going out with you this summer, so you're dumped."

I raced towards the portables, pretending I needed something from my purse, and I guess I did, because that's where

crushed

I kept my little travel pack of tissues (as all fancy ladies do). I raced in and began rummaging through my purse only to hear footsteps behind me and then a low voice, a voice not quite grown-up but definitely hitting puberty a full eighteen months before the other boys.

"Hey, you're too pretty to be crying."

"Logan?"

Logan was the only boy in school history to get detention on the first day. He also may have been a legal adult in fifth grade, I don't know…but he had just called me pretty.

"I just got dumped."

"Well, would you like to go out with me?"

Tears were still streaming down my cheeks, my nose still sniffling as I enthusiastically yelped, "Okay!"

The next day at recess was amazing, until I realized I had left my friendship bracelet making string in my purse (which I had forgotten in the portable yet again). I stepped inside to see Logan already at my desk.

Oh my goodness, he's leaving me love notes already!

"Wait, why are you holding my purse?"

"Well, you carry a purse, and you were so upset yesterday I knew you'd be easy to steal from."

⁕⁕⁕

Fifth grade wasn't all bad because I won Best Actress for our school play. Unlike that whole recess MASH incident, my professional life was going places.

I mean, sure, I was cast as Bill Sikes in *Oliver!* (hello, full circle), and sure, that's a boy character, and sure, the popular

kiersten lyons

girls whose moms let them get perms made fun of me for it (especially when they stippled on a beard), but I was also a big deal. Huge! Teachers told me to remember them when I got famous, grown-ups were asking my parents if they were going to get me an agent, and first graders were asking for my autograph. Sure, the kids my age didn't care, but they would soon…because I was going to be famous.

This was my way out, my chance to prove to Kevin and Matty, to Ryan and Terrence, to every single popular girl with a perm, to John and my freaking older brother that they were wrong about me!

Famous people aren't ugly or gross, they aren't unlovable or losers, and they definitely aren't forgettable (over a summer or at all!). I had a plan, I had a purpose, and I was going to prove them all wrong!

Well, everyone except for Logan. I wasn't sure how to prove that I wasn't easy to steal from.

Please let me know if you have any ideas.

Chapter Ten

late bloomer

The summer before sixth grade (a.k.a. my last year in elementary school), I decided to cut my hair short again, or as my dad called it: the "Dorothy Hamill." A bunch of girls on the swim team (including a girl my brother's age, so I knew it was cool) were doing it, so I was all, "I will do anything to be cool and part of the group, so let's do this!"

But those girls had blow-dryers and giant curling brushes, and they were allowed to use hairspray (I had lost that privilege a year before when I emptied a whole bottle of Aqua Net on my hair minutes before my Aunt Ginny was to walk down the aisle).

But also, what do you expect, Mom, after you left it within reach?!

What I'm saying is they had style, and I had...another bowl cut. Which wasn't doing much for my self-esteem as puberty began to greet all my friends but stayed entirely away from me. Well, not entirely—Lauren's mom took her to get training bras at JCPenney and let me tag along.

kiersten lyons

Gloria was the coolest mom. She was a full decade younger than my mom, listened to the 107.3 The Hits music station, and had a tennis racket earring in one ear.

Just one ear, people!

So, while my mom was busy telling me I could never use hairspray again, Gloria said, "Kiersten, why don't you pick out a little training bra too?"

And if you're wondering, yes, I proceeded to tug at that bra every chance I got so that Matty (yup, he's still around) would see that I was wearing one and therefore must be mature enough for a relationship. He didn't notice, so I pulled out my final card, the one I'd been holding for some time now. The one I knew would make him mine.

"Hey, Matty?"

"Yeah?"

"I can recite the fifty states in alphabetical order in less than twenty seconds."

We had learned the banger that was "Fifty Nifty United States" at some point during our hallowed education, and I was sure my knowledge and quickness would impress him. It did, so much so he brought over his girlfriend, a.k.a. the most popular girl, to my desk, so I could do it for her too.

As elementary school came to a close, I got a lovely gift for graduation: a large bag of Maxi-pads my mom put up in my closet. All summer those pads stared back at me, taunting me, telling me I wouldn't be any sort of a woman or be cool until I used one. I wish I could tell you I used one that summer, but alas, they stayed there…for four more years.

crushed

My first day of seventh grade was...

Wait—before we move on, I feel like we need a check-in of sorts. I mean, I'm about to walk into Martin Luther King Jr. Middle School, and we all know how deeply uncomplicated middle school halls are, and you're about to walk in with me, so how you doing? Having any bits of clarity?

None for me—thanks for asking.

Definitely no correlation between my big brother being mean to me and the type of boys I'm attracted to. Plus, I had my three younger siblings to take care of, not only because I loved them, but also because my mom had another psychotic break before middle school (or maybe it was the year before?), but that's not super important. What is important is I love taking care of others and the feeling I get when I sacrifice my whole self to do it! (Bonus: this is not at all a trauma response and more so another wonderful way to validate my worth!)

So many of my teachers (and swim coaches and theater directors) would see me with my siblings and go on and on about how I would make such a great teacher, which all at once delighted me (because compliments) and infuriated me. Sure, I loved kids, but had they not seen my perfect MASH board for my perfect life?!

kiersten lyons

My 13 year old PERFECT ♥ MASH ♥

Marry:
Jonathan Taylor
Thomas

City:
NY, NY

Job:
Broadway Actress

Kids:
Four

My Reader's PERFECT ♥ MASH ♥

Marry:

City:

Job:

Kids:

crushed

I mean, did these grown-ups not understand the plan? There was one choice, and one choice only, to reach the goal!

I rehearsed the goal often; my twin bed would magically transform to *The Tonight Show* couch where Jay and I would banter back and forth (this was years before Jimmy). I'd tell a quippy tale or two and then he'd ask me if I had anything else to say before he cut to commercial. And then, all casual, like super chill, I would just look into the camera, raise one eyebrow, and say without a care in the world, "What now, Matty?"

Which is exactly what I was envisioning that first day of seventh grade, as he laughed at me. Oh, no, not Matty, or even John, but the boy who would take up this fantasy for the next six years (and then some). It happened a few periods into the first day...

Not to be confused with my first period, which was probably never going to come.

I was desperately trying to get my locker opened—seriously, who invented locks with their "hit the number on the first spin, but don't you dare do the same motion on the second, no GO PAST the number and then abruptly swing back, but then you better hit it a third time PERFECTLY, and if you don't, well, then start over, you loser!" Anyway, I was on my fourth try, tears beginning to well up, when I looked over to see the girl with the locker next to mine possibly conceiving a baby with her boyfriend. Horrified (but also very much intrigued), I backed away, right into...

"I hate when I run into walls. Get it? Cause she's flat."

Everybody laughed.

kiersten lyons

His name was Lyndsay, and sure, most would say it's a girl name, but somehow not one person in our school ever caught on to that. I blame his popularity, his cute face that screamed "I'm going to be captain of the lacrosse team a few years from now," and his sharp ability to make sure everyone around him felt just a little bit lesser than him.

I immediately pulled up my binder to cover my chest (a move I would continue until halfway through senior year) and quickly ran to my next class, tears welling up. I shut my eyes tight, reminding myself about the couch, about the camera, about the moment when he'd know just how wrong he was.

I perfected this move over the next few months: walking through the halls physically, but mentally in Hollywood, mentally everyone finally knowing I had worth, mentally me finally knowing I had worth, until as fate would have it, Lyndsay and I climbed onto the exact same after school activity bus.

Oh my gosh, he's sitting directly diagonally to me...

There was one other kid near us. His name was Nate, and he had thick glasses and a raw clown-like smile. Literally, his lips were chapped for an extra quarter inch around his entire mouth. Lyndsay looked over at me.

I think he's going to say something to me.

"You got any chapstick?"

"Um...no."

Why don't you have chapstick, Kiersten?! This was your chance!

crushed

"You sure you don't have any chapstick? Because somebody could really use some chapstick." His eyes darted to Nate, then back to me, as he wryly smiled.

That smile.

I knew I had two choices: one, I could go along with Lyndsay, and he would become my boyfriend right then and there (no *Tonight Show* couch moment needed), or two, I could ignore his taunting, but then he wouldn't be my first kiss, so I...

"I know. I can't believe how poor people are that they can't afford chapstick!"

We talked about chapstick for the next eleven minutes until the bus abruptly stopped, and then just as abruptly, Lyndsay got off.

Oh, he's probably going to put his number on a note and then sail it through the window on a paper airplane. That is so much more romantic than just asking for—

But he just walked off, no look back, not even a wave. I mean, who talks about chapstick with someone for the length of half an episode of *Saved by the Bell* and then pretends like it didn't even happen?! A boy that will spend the next six years tormenting me by mostly being cruel, but occasionally showing me attention, that's who.

At least with Kevin I got a new career opportunity, but this? This felt different. Somehow worse. Why? And how?

I made the mistake of looking back at Nick: his eyes were as red as his lips. I sat next to him for the next ten minutes. Possibly the longest ten minutes of my life: because it was at that moment I realized, for the first time, I had the ability to crush others.

Except here's the thing about clarity, the thing about writing it down: it can unlock some core memory shit. Because this wasn't the first time. The first time was two years before.

Let's call him Ivan, and he was tough to have in class; what we now know as emotional dysregulation was back then just known as a kid who blew up all the time. It didn't help he was small, and it didn't help that he was a loner, but for whatever reason the boys that bullied me thought it would be funny to tell everyone I liked him.

How could they do this? He's the weirdest boy in class, and no matter what I say, these boys keep saying it.

Comedy was king in my house, and my dad was the best joke teller in the neighborhood, maybe the world, and when you made him laugh, you'd know you were big time. But to make my big brother, Luke, laugh? Oh, that was selling out at Madison Square Garden kind of fame. It didn't happen often for me, but when it did, it was pure gold. For just a second, I wasn't a loser or an inbred (yeah, this is something Luke would call me often, which was particularly confusing to me because we obviously had the same parents).

Dummy.

Anyway, at those dinner tables where I was learning timing and how to wait for a laugh, I was also learning insults, because oftentimes the comedy got hurtful, and my

crushed

mom would go, "Barry!" and he would go, "I'm just kidding. Kiersten knows I'm kidding."

I did, but also, did I?

Nuance when you're eleven is confusing, but not confusing is the pride I got when I made them all laugh.

Which brings me to Ivan and the other boys (and girls) that wouldn't stop making fun of me because, "He's a dork, you're a dork—you're perfect together!"

In one afternoon, I used two comedy tenets I didn't even know I was using: satire and "yes, and," and I did them both beautifully.

Because I wrote a pretend secret admirer letter to Ivan, joking about all the things I loved about him—his ability to have a temper tantrum so easily, his curly hair (he actually had great hair, so I'm not really sure what I was trying to say here), and all the other things about him that made him so charming. It was my way of changing the narrative, of pushing back, of getting the laugh.

He was never supposed to see it; it was only for my friends. But my boy fifth-grade teacher's co-teacher, Ms. Lewy (yeah, we switched halfway through each day because that's how grown-up we were in the portables) saw me passing it and grabbed it from my hands.

"NO!"

Sternly she opened it up. "We don't pass notes in class."

I asked her to read it first. I was sure she'd see the comedy in it, but also how cruel it could be if it was read out loud. But she waved me off and began reading. Out loud. To the *entire class.*

kiersten lyons

Ivan's head immediately dropped. He knew it wasn't a real love note (I'm not sure how, but something tells me despite his struggles with behavioral management, he was aware and super sensitive). She kept reading until she realized the class was laughing and Ivan was crying. She was angry, looking back perhaps mostly at herself (like seriously, why do teachers think reading notes aloud will do anything but cause us years in therapy?!), and ushered the class out for specials—I think it was music.

But Ivan wouldn't budge. Like I had seen so many times before, he glued himself to that seat, refusing to listen to directions, except this time I knew exactly why.

So, I refused to leave too, everything in me could care less about the laugh, could care less that the other kids could probably see, but I went up to his desk and crouched down. I tried to tell him how sorry I was, how even though I thought he would never see it, it still wasn't okay to write.

Tears were still on his cheeks as I teared up too, realizing how deeply I had hurt someone in the same way I had been hurt so many times before. I told him I liked his curly hair (which was so true!) and how unfair it was to make fun of it. I felt eyes on me and realized Ms. Lewy had left the portable door open, so the entire class lined up outside saw me crouching down, telling Ivan how much I liked his curly hair, but I didn't care. I promised myself I would never hurt someone that way again.

And yet, I did…

Chapter Eleven

status update—still a late bloomer

Just in case you were wondering, Sam G. telling you that you are a flat-chested alien is no fun.

Actually, Sam didn't even tell me—he looked straight past me to ask the guy who I had just slow danced with why he wasted a dance on the loud, annoying flat girl with the alien eyes and giant alien head.

What I'm saying is middle school was just more of the same. More chances for me to shut my eyes and be on that *Tonight Show* couch, more chances for me to pour everything I had into the future when Sam G. and Lyndsay and every single one of those popular girls would finally see how wrong they were!

There were some glimmers of hope, like meeting my first Mormon and him telling me I had good birthing hips. Oh, and getting cast as the lead in *Oliver*. Yes, *Oliver*.

Is there any other show a school will do?

kiersten lyons

But this time I got vindication, because this time I was cast as Nancy!

She's a girl!

Also, quite vindicating? I fell for the Artful Dodger, and guess what? That Artful Dodger fell for me too! During an especially exciting math class I was passed a tiny football-shaped paper note asking if I would go out with him. *Check yes, no, or maybe.*

YES!

But then he kept coming to all my classes and wanting to carry my books and calling my house, like...all the time.

"Mom, can you just tell him I'm not home?"

"Kiersten, I don't think you want a boyfriend. I think what you want is a boy you like and can chase, and then he just tells the whole school he likes you back."

Just because you go to therapy doesn't mean you know me, woman!

And she said all of this as she reached into my closet to grab a pad. Oh, no, not for me; in a fit of panic, she needed to borrow one. I mean, how rude can one person be?!

But you know who wasn't rude? John.

During intermission of opening night of *Oliver!* he raced downstairs to find me.

"Kiersten, you're like, good. Really good! Your voice—I had no idea you could sing like that! You're going to be so famous! I'm going to be your biggest fan—no, I'm going to be your manager!"

And from that day forward, he came to all my shows, and he never let anyone on the football team mess with me. That's

crushed

not to say they wouldn't try, but if he was around, he'd say, "Be careful, she's going to be famous."

Fame wasn't just so people could see how wrong they were; it was protection. It was where I would finally feel safe.

I entered my freshman year with three goals: to become a Thespian (the honor society for actors, named after Thespis, the first actor, naturally), to get my first kiss, and to use the freaking bag of pads!

How dare my body betray me like this?!!

And it only got worse as high school swim practice began. At least once a practice, a girl would walk just a little bit ahead of the group and embarrassingly ask, "Girls, can you see my string?" I would become enraged with jealousy, until one day I began lying. Every week or so I would ask, very convincingly, "Girls, can you see my string?" I obviously didn't understand the whole once-a-month thing just yet.

Then, on February 10, 1997, nine days before I turned sixteen and halfway through my sophomore year I asked, "Girls, can you see my string?" and finally wasn't lying! But as I was just approaching puberty, my friends were approaching something entirely more grown-up.

"Mom, all my friends are having sex, they're all making love, and I haven't even been kissed yet!" (To be fair, it was only one friend who was doing it, but I had too many emotions, and this was not a time for clarity!)

kiersten lyons

My mom was calm, looking at me with all the compassion of a woman who's probably talked this very moment out with her therapist many times before.

"Kiersten, your friends aren't having sex, and they're certainly not making love. They're fucking. That's all they're doing—just fucking."

You just heard her, right?

I had never in my life heard my mom swear, let alone use the F word. I mean, this is the woman who made us go to church every Sunday, even on vacation!

"Kiersten, it's not cursing—it's stating a fact. They don't understand the gravitas with what they do."

I mean, yes, my parents were holy, but they were also honest—and not just with that book with the cartoon sperm. No, my dad was always very open about how he was when he was younger. Because my dad was…well, you see, my dad was a bit of player. He was…okay, fine. My dad was a slut. His words.

"Kiersten, these boys think about sex every minute of the day. They're doing the best they can with their hormones."

Like an athlete training, I reviewed the tapes, as in the VHS of *Grease* (stop worrying—my parents made me fast forward the car make-out scene). *Grease* was the pinnacle, a cinematic masterpiece. It had a cool boy who was mean to a girl until he realized he was being mean to her because he loved her! Plus, she wasn't giving it up, and HE STILL LOVED HER (even after she slammed his private parts with the car door). There was singing and dancing, her getting a hot girl makeover, him changing his bad boy ways for

crushed

her, and then both of them driving off into the clouds in a shiny car.

I wasn't giving it up—I mean, I asked for a purity ring for my seventeenth birthday. I was waiting until marriage! I just wanted to have the *ability* to say no. To be able to slam one car door on a guy's privates at the drive-in movie, and then he'd sing a song about me. To have just one guy who liked me enough to lie to my face and try and get in my pants…I wasn't even good enough to lie to.

Chapter Twelve

growing up

His name was Chris, and he had muscles. Real muscles! I was growing up, and so was my type; no more scrawny guys for me. (Okay, he also had blond hair and blue eyes, but still, look at me maturing!)

There were only two problems: we didn't go to the same school, and we actually hadn't talked. I just saw him onstage at the Maryland State Thespian Festival and knew he was the one (as is the beginning of every major romance).

He was cute, a theater kid, and upon my in-depth investigation (i.e., talking to other theater kids he went to school with), I found out he didn't drink or smoke. CAN YOU EVEN BELIEVE IT?!

One of those girls thought Chris and I would be great together (obviously a very intelligent gal) and gave me his number. I began to devise a plan, one where I would call him and be all, "Oh, my gosh, yeah, we totally met. You don't remember?!" (My investigation also led me to find out he was a bit forgetful.) But on the morning of my planned call, as I

crushed

was getting ready in the bathroom, I heard my dad say to my mom, "MaryPat, I always appreciate your honesty."

I realized I couldn't start our relationship on false pretenses, so I did the next best thing: I went to Kohl's and blew all my lifeguarding money on some hot new numbers that I wore to the High School Theater Festival that summer in Williamsburg, Virginia. Because what says theater more than watching a guy dressed as a blacksmith make horseshoes?

A few days into the trip, he asked me to be his partner on a rollercoaster (Chris, not the pretend blacksmith). I absolutely hated roller coasters.

I said yes.

The picture the ride took was just me staring at him. At $19.95, I didn't have enough money (see: *Kohl's*), but at $4.95, I *did* have enough for the tiny viewfinder keychain picture of the entire group.

"Mom, do you wanna see Chris again? He's the one in the top row, third from the left. No, Mom, you gotta close your left eye tighter, so then you can see him better with your right."

Ugh, parents and technology, am I right?

Us theater kids hung out together all the time, and a couple months later I met his mom.

"Oh, *you're* Kiersten," she said pleasantly.

Oh my gosh, he told his mom about me. Obviously, I can now ask him to my homecoming.

I dialed his number, my heart racing faster with each ring, because it wasn't his cell (we wouldn't all have those for a few more years); no, the year was 1997, and when you called a boy, it was at his house, and you'd never know who would pick up.

SERIOUSLY IT COULD BE ANYONE!

"Hello?"

"Oh, hi, um, this is Kiersten. Is Chris there?"

"Oh, hello sweetie. Let me get him."

She loves me.

"Hello?"

"Hi, Chris, it's Kiersten. I was wondering if you, um…if you wanted to go to homecoming with me?"

The phone was silent. Too silent. I had to break the tension. I had to be chill.

"As friends—like, just as friends."

"Yeah, sure, that'd be cool."

crushed

Homecoming was magical. I mean, I had the cutest guy by far, so Lyndsay who? (Just kidding, you best believe I looked around often to see if Lyndsay was looking, you know, for research purposes.) As Chris walked me to my door, we lingered, and then he...hugged me. But I was sure the kiss was coming the next weekend at my fall play.

I was one of the leads, had a New York accent, and within minutes heard Chris's distinct laugh in the audience. After the curtain call, I raced past family and friends to find him. We hugged, even longer this time.

"Thank you for coming to my show."

"Yeah, you were funny."

Funny's good. Funny leads to relationship banter.

"Kiersten, I wanted to introduce you to someone. This is my shy, sweet, and nothing-at-all-like-you girlfriend, Katie."

Okay—maybe those weren't his exact words, but that's what I heard.

"Your girlfriend? You have a girlfriend? Oh, that's amazing."

I waited until I got to my friend's car before I completely lost it, which was only made worse by the fact she turned on Mix 107.3 The Hits and "My Heart Will Go On" was playing. I felt just like Leo, in icy waters with no room on the door....

But a twist I didn't see coming? That Artful Dodger—you know, the one from eighth grade who wouldn't stop calling? Well, we never stopped doing theater together—he even went to all those theater festivals too. And guess what? He liked a girl from Chris's school, but she didn't like him back either. We commiserated together, talking about our broken hearts for hours, until we stopped talking about them and just talked.

And one afternoon, halfway through my junior year, while backstage during a dress rehearsal for *Into the Woods*, he dressed as Cinderella's Prince and I in the Witch's second act costume (you know, after she wasn't old and scary anymore) kissed.

I had heard of first kisses being gross or awkward, but mine was sweet, with one of my best friends. Suddenly, being a late bloomer wasn't all that bad. So much so that a lovely young man who I had gone to school with since third grade wrote this on the back of his senior picture to me.

crushed

Why yes, it does say, "Horribly deformed and ugly."

He was also best friends with Lyndsay, and by graduation, they all had become some sort of amalgam—the whole lot of them becoming a large conglomerate I needed to prove wrong. The final days of senior year I was voted "Most Likely to Become Famous," my future now publicly carved in stone. I couldn't get to my *The Tonight Show* fast enough.

I had to wait just a bit, as my parents didn't support the idea of me moving to a big ol' city just yet—something about me not being mature enough.

Oh, but I was mature enough to basically take on the emotional labor of the whole house for most of my formative years?!

It's fine! I definitely don't have built up resentment that I won't fully process for another two decades about all that.

Another thing I probably needed to process: the fact that a boy I liked, *really* liked me back. Just after graduation I started talking to a boy from Chris's school. Two problems: I was leaving for college in eight weeks, and he was younger (but somehow the most mature boy I'd met up until this point). He was funny and honest and kind.

Wait…kind? That's weird….

Just like the Artful Dodger, he kept showing up—except not with phone calls, but handwritten letters. For most of the summer he was a camp counselor, which meant once a week I would get a handwritten letter.

And I kid you not, every single time I went to the mailbox, it was raining, and yes, thank you for asking, I was basically Rachel McAdams in *The Notebook*. Except as sweet as our little summer romance was, filled with innocence and making each other laugh, it was just that—summer. He still had two years back home, and I had no time for getting caught in Maryland, caught in love.

You've seen my MASH!

Plus, having a boy I liked, who just automatically liked me back, was too easy. It didn't make sense.

I've memorized You've Got Mail; *I know how much back and forth, how much fighting needs to happen before he realizes he loves me...*

I went to a small liberal arts school where the two biggest majors were musical theater and pre-med (which truly made for an incredible hybrid of community). I kept my purity ring intact, I got cast in some great productions while I was there, and I joined a sorority. Mostly because that's what cool girls did, and I don't know if you've been following along, but a cool girl is all I want to be!

And when I say "kept my purity ring intact," I'm not joking—first week of freshman year, some guys in my dorm found out about the ring, and within weeks there was a bet on who could get it first. At one point the bet was apparently up to $1,200. I know I should've been offended, but for a late bloomer like me, I loved the shit out of that attention! I was basically the Temu version of *She's All That*.

Speaking of attention, I caught the eye of a frat president, and throughout my freshman year, we bantered back and forth, he understanding I wasn't going to sleep with anybody,

crushed

me loving to drop some witty comment as we passed each other and then being on my way. It was like we were in the first act of our very own romcom, and it was *the best*.

At the end of the year, his fraternity hosted a party for the last night of classes, and I found myself pretending to not know how to spit.

Wait, that sounded so much dirtier than I intended.

Okay, so remember that scene in *Titanic* where Leo teaches Kate how to properly spit? Of course you do. Well, that was him teaching me how to spit off the frat house's balcony. I don't even know how we got to that point, but I do know that I already knew how to "hock a loogie" but pretended I didn't, so he could teach me. We kissed for the first time later that night.

What the hell is up with us pretending we don't know how to do something so the guy feels important?

Upon learning I had a huge crush on Ben Affleck, he chose a movie night for our third date. *Armageddon*, naturally. We talked through most of it, joking around (and occasionally making out). It was perfect, until he pressed pause.

"Wait, this is the best part. I don't want you to miss it."

I had already seen the movie but pretended I hadn't (seriously, WHAT IS UP WITH US DOING THIS?!). Frat President pressed play just as Ben put animal crackers on Liv Tyler's stomach. She asked something like, "Do you think anyone is doing what we're about to do right now?"

And Ben Affleck goes, "I hope so, baby, or what are we going up there for?"

kiersten lyons

FB (what I shall now call Frat President because I don't want to keep typing out that long of a name) paused the movie again. "Well?"

"Well, what?"

"He makes a good point, don't you think?"

I laughed thinking he was being funny, but his face said otherwise. Why I didn't break it off right then? I mean obviously he had a terrible sense of humor, and for a guy in pre-med, he wasn't all that bright. I mean, *these* were his moves?!

It didn't matter—within weeks, he realized Ben or not, I wasn't budging, so he ghosted me. Full stop on texting or calling.

This doesn't make any sense at all. I stood up for myself!

Guys love when a girl is all, "Who do you think you are?" I mean, your girl metaphorically slammed the car door on FB's crotch. He should've turned to camera and belted out a song all about how much he loved me. I shouldn't have been left on read!

After that, I did what any gal in the year 2000 would: made one of my friends AOL Instant Message him and be all, "Hey, did you hear Kiersten's in New York right now for an audition to be Tom Hank's daughter in his new movie?"

Guess who got a text right after.

Hey, I heard you're in New York?

Did it matter that Tom Hanks that year (or any of the close years following) did not have a movie where he had a daughter my age? No, because one, we've already established FB wasn't the brightest, and two, it only solidified everything

crushed

I already knew to be true—being famous will take away the pain.

I left college after my sophomore year. It wasn't that I didn't believe in education—it was just that if I stayed for the next two years to graduate, I was going to be accruing $60,000 in student loans to then move out to become a struggling actress, and I figured, "Hey, let's cut out that whole debt thing and get out with two more years of youth!"

Plus, my school was all about the theater (you're not pronouncing it right: it's *theatre*!), and my love was the sitcom (Jodie Sweetin already knew this). So where is the most logical place for a twenty-one-year-old virgin actress to go?

You guessed it: Hollywood, California.

Chapter Thirteen

la la land

Right before moving to LA, two major things happened: one, my mom made me watch a ton of *E! True Hollywood Story* episodes because she wanted me to be prepared for the rejection, the casting couches, and what really goes on in Tinseltown. You know—show business!

I knew much of these stories already as my dad had been a junior agent for a few months in the '70s and told tales about dropping off scripts to actors' homes, how cutthroat the business was, and of course, "all the cocaine." My dad had experience with addiction in his family, so he wanted nothing to do with the last one but made sure to let me know about all the giant bowls of cocaine that decorated Hollywood parties. (Side note: I've been to a ton of Hollywood parties and I've never once seen a bowl, giant or otherwise, of cocaine just laying about.)

The other major one? I found out weeks before moving that my homecoming date Chris had just moved there, too. I hadn't kept tabs on him since leaving high school.

crushed

Well, unless you count taping his Abercrombie bags next to our homecoming photos on the walls of my dorm room. Which I don't!

Suffice it to say, this was obviously fate stepping in to confirm that we were really and truly perfect for each other.

I packed up my car with a tiny dresser full of my high school Kohl's haul (and a smattering of J. Crew clearance from college) and all the gumption a girl who had been voted "Most Likely to Become Famous" could have.

Okay, before we officially get on the road to LA, we have an update to my perfect MASH, and it needs to be documented:

No longer was JTT my main squeeze. I mean, sure I was moving to LA, and sure he was there, but I had grown up, literally. I was now a few inches taller than him, but also, I was a mature girl of twenty-one; I understood that knowing someone in real life was very different than learning about them through magazine articles curated by a PR person. Thus, it was time for someone real to hold that space. And it wasn't just romantic partners I was maturing about, either: In college, I recognized Broadway wasn't an attainable dream. Even with a strong belt, I couldn't sight read and struggled with harmonies, so the bright lights of Broadway had to be swapped for the bright lights of Hollywood—which honestly made perfect sense. Much easier to get famous this way.

And just in case you too had some realizations since middle school, I'll leave you a blank MASH board to update.

kiersten lyons

My 21 year old PERFECT

♥ ~~MASH~~ ♥

Marry:

Chris Carmack

City:

Hollywood

Job:

Famous Actress

Kids:

Three

My Reader's PERFECT

♥ MASH ♥

Marry:

City:

Job:

Kids:

crushed

I'm twenty-one now, people, a full woman who's got her life fully figured out! Obviously this MASH is permanent.

And I was so right. Within months of arriving to LA, I had an incredible agent, the seggsiest of headshots, and after just three auditions, I booked my first major guest star on network TV!

Just kidding. Within months of arriving, I accidentally joined a Christian cult.

Right before I moved to LA, I found a cute garage apartment for rent online and put a down payment on it, sight unseen. I wasn't just watching *E! True Hollywood Story*, I was fire hosing myself in all things E! Entertainment Television, and one day came across a one-off documentary about a girl right around my age who had booked the lead in a new sitcom for the WB (you know, before all that CW nonsense). The actress lived in Burbank and worked at Warner Brothers Studio, which was also in Burbank, so naturally I made it my mission to move to Burbank (where all the fanciest people lived!).

What the family didn't tell me about their garage apartment was that they only converted about one-third of it. You know, one of those, "your wingspan is the width of the apartment" kind of places. I was shocked when I saw the size, but the owners were sweet and had an adorable eighteen-month-old who I loved, and this all helped me to not feel so homesick. Within minutes of meeting, the owner was gushing about her church that was filled with young people all pursuing the same dreams as me (well, the acting part, not the getting Chris to fall in love with them part).

kiersten lyons

To be fair, I was playing it super chill with Chris anyway. And by super chill, yes, I do mean texting him the minute I drove across the state line into California and then making sure I was completely available the second he asked to hang out.

That evening, I drove from my Burbank apartment to his spacious Hollywood one to meet up with him and his director roommate and head to quintessential LA burger spot In-N-Out. Mr. Roommate Director Man wasn't some "I want to be a director," but an "I already have an Academy Award for Best Documentary," which was currently starring at me, as I did my best not to stare at Chris. I was obviously already nervous for this whole hang out shebang but seeing that Oscar on the mantel brought a whole new level of anxiety I couldn't shake no matter how many In-N-Out fries I stuffed my face with. Which I was doing when Mr. Roommate Director Man suggested we all see a film.

Yes, I did say film. No, Cheryl, it's not called a movie, this is Hollywood! Where we see films with subtitles and super segssy nekkid scenes which totally do not make me uncomfortable. Look how I make my face look so bored as I watch this film, so everyone knows how normal and everyday this all is for me.

As we were leaving the tiny indie theater (WE DO NOT SEE FILMS IN CHAIN MOVIE THEATERS, CHERYL), Mr. Roommate Director Man noticed some producer friends were also there, so we all popped across the street to grab sushi "because we have got to talk about what we just experienced."

I would soon learn this is all anyone does in LA—talk about films. Ad nauseum.

crushed

Oh, and sushi? No, it's definitely not my first time. Yeah, I do this all the time. Because I'm cool and chill and super breezy.

A server who had already perfected her bored look dropped a plate of what I would learn was called edamame on the table. One of the producers immediately grabbed a pod of beans and popped it in his mouth, everyone else following suit. With all the confidence of a girl who definitely eats sushi all the time, I did as well. The producers began going over the film with a fine-tooth comb, but all I could do was chew.

How is everybody so easily able to eat theirs?

And that's when I saw the shells on the second plate and realized, in horror, that they hadn't popped the full thing in their mouth, just the beans!

At this point the producers and Mr. Roommate Director Man were finding symbolism in places I'm pretty sure it wasn't but I couldn't say anything BECAUSE I WAS STILL CHEWING! I tried to hide my face behind the menu...

Maybe I can just spit it out in a napkin...

The bored server hadn't dropped napkins yet! As my entire future flashed before my eyes—I realized my only choice was to swallow the pod whole so Chris (and what felt like the entire entertainment industry sitting in the booth) would never notice what a loser I was. And so I did, praying the entire time that no one would notice I had no idea what I was doing.

But you know what I did have an idea about? God.

From the moment I entered my landlord's church (well, a nightclub they rented out on Wednesday nights and Sunday

kiersten lyons

mornings), I was surrounded by attractive people in their twenties who were kind and welcoming, and within one day I already had plans with new friends. And for a girl who only had one friend in town and was missing her family something fierce, this was amazing. Soon I was invited to go to cool late-night diners, bowling, horseback riding, and the most LA thing of all: brunch.

There is nothing like brunch in LA, mostly because at any morning slash early afternoon you can find one. It isn't like other towns where brunch is only for the weekends. Nope, in LA, brunch is always and everywhere (mostly because so many of us work evening shifts at restaurants or live off commercial residuals, or if you're hot you are given a tiny tank top and packs of free shaving cream to promote a brand's new peach scent on the Santa Monica promenade to make rent. What I'm saying is: it's a weird town).

It was at one such brunch that I was casually invited to a Bible study. I accepted and that's when the casualness stopped. They told me it was Tuesday; I told them I already had plans with my friend Chris and I would catch the next one. That wasn't possible, they explained. This Tuesday was the study. Everyone looked around at each other, as my closest friend (and the only one who knew of my future wedding plans) leaned in and whispered that sometimes it's a good idea to not always be available.

Solid point...

As Tuesday approached, I texted for the address but was told they were coming to me, which was odd since I was the one being *invited* (and also I lived in a third of a garage),

crushed

but sure. Tuesday came but my friends did not—just two random girls I'd never seen before, one quiet, one very not quiet. No, but seriously, the quiet one introduced herself then never spoke again. Like ever. She just watched the other one, almost as if she was being trained. I asked if my friends were running late, but talking girl said it would just be the three of us, and I was so confused; I thought this was the night they always had Bible study? I had changed plans with Chris!

Do they even realize what a big deal it is to change plans with your future husband who actually doesn't know he's your future husband yet?!

This was starting to become more confusing than the edamame because I understood Bible stuff and what was happening in my tiny apartment as one girl talked and the other looked like someone had told her to never speak again *was not it.*

Talking girl began forcefully flipping my Bible to random verses throughout the Old and New Testament, pulling out a sentence or half a sentence and then having me read it out loud, helping me to understand how truly terrible of a person I was. She would ask me a question that felt accusatory even when I hadn't answered, and more than once she explained I wasn't part of the kingdom yet, and until I was, I was a terrible sinner going to hell.

The kingdom apparently meant getting baptized. When I explained I was, they told me it had to be in their church for it count towards the kingdom.

It was such a 180, a crazy whiplash from the kindness, the welcome, the sweet friends I had made over the last month

kiersten lyons

or so. By the time they left I was almost shaking, feeling so defensive, yet scared: Was I about to lose all my new friends? Did I need to get baptized in their kingdom or whatever, so I wouldn't be alone? I was three thousand miles away from family, and I was in a new city trying to become an actress and failing miserably—in a word, I was vulnerable.

I told my landlord what had happened, she immediately got a woman named Lisa on the phone. Lisa's husband was a pastor, and she was kind of the head of the young women at the church. By the time I got to church on Wednesday night, Lisa gently held my shoulders and apologized profusely for everything that happened. She assured me she would talk to both girls and invited me over to a Bible study at *her* house that she'd be having in a couple of weeks, promising all my new friends who were so lovely would be there too.

I felt relieved and called my parents. I had been filling them in on all my new adventures, especially about the church—I knew they'd be happy I had found quality people in the land of cocaine in a bowl. They sounded concerned, and not just about the aggressive Bible study. They gently noticed that I was spending all my time with these people—church twice a week, plus almost every night doing something.

"You haven't mentioned Chris in weeks."

I got defensive. Chris was great, obviously, and I had big plans with him, but on the other hand, the church kept telling me about the kind of guy I should be with, and maybe they were right. I mean, there were so many successful marriages in it, many couples who seemed so in love.

crushed

They raised me to know Jesus, now I'm meeting others who do, and they're concerned about it? Do they not understand that if I leave now, I'll have nothing and no one?!

Plus, the only way I could've even met a guy in the church was to get baptized there; you could talk to boys, sure, but you absolutely could not get into a relationship with one or even go on a date until you were both in the kingdom. I had a friend who liked a cute boy, and Lisa had finally approved for them to date.

I want that chance!

Over the next week, my parents overnighted me a book about theology and begged me to read it.

"Kiersten, you don't have to believe what we do. You're an adult. Your faith is your own. But some of the things you've brought up, like the money, for instance…it might be a good thing to get a different opinion."

Fine, whatever. I love you guys; I'll read your stupid book.

I really wasn't sure what they were so concerned about. My family tithed every month (10 percent to the church and worthy causes) and oftentimes much more. My parents were super generous with those around them. My dad would often see someone asking for money on the street and walk up to them, have a chat, and ask their food order.

"Kiersten, every person deserves the dignity of getting to choose what they'd like to eat."

This church did the same thing; people there gave 10 percent, and then this other thing I'd only heard rumbles around—something called *specials*. I didn't know enough

kiersten lyons

about it, but it seemed like another opportunity to give, another opportunity to offer dignity.

Plus, there were cute boys there who actually liked that I was waiting until marriage. What the hell was my parents' problem?!

My best friend invited me to her rehab graduation—well, the church's form of rehab: an intensive, months-long journey to go through all your past wrongs and take account for them all while sharing all your darkest secrets in front of many other people. Hearing the graduates' struggles felt confusing—my dad's sister was a recovering drug addict, and addiction runs pretty rampant in my family. I can't diagnose a person one way or another, but many of these people's stories sounded non-addictive, almost as if someone was telling them they were something perhaps they really weren't. I overheard someone saying that a pastor told him he couldn't be baptized or part of the kingdom until he went through this program. It felt controlling, but I pushed that thought away, not wanting to lose my community.

There was one more tidbit: I had taken a job on Rodeo Drive working days (as opposed to keep trying to get a restaurant job) because my friends at the church encouraged me that it would offer me more opportunities to grow closer to God. I would have my evenings free for Wednesday night church, prayer times, hangouts, and, of course, Bible study.

"Maybe God put it on your heart to become an actress to really come out here and find our church. Maybe it was never about acting and always about finding this place."

crushed

The first time I heard this, I thought it sounded so purposeful, and coupled with this new community that would do anything for me, it all made sense. But I was now repeating the same words to my parents weeks later, doing my best to defend the church to them. And myself...

"Sweetie, did the book arrive?" my mom asked.

"It did today."

"Please read it."

I heard the concern in her voice, and it was the same concern bubbling up in me. The rehab graduation was one chip, and then a few nights later, Lisa made a comment about me not attending the Wednesday night prayer service. Something about not putting the proper things in the proper order. It felt accusatory and not at all loving. And then I learned what *specials* were...

They called it an "opportunity" for those in the kingdom to give an extra 20 or 30 percent of their income (I can't remember exactly) to the church they loved so dearly. Please note, this is on top of the 10 percent they were already made to give to be part of the kingdom. Some held garage sales, others took on a second job, and one girl bought cheap NSYNC t-shirts at the dollar store and sold them on the street outside a concert.

While I could appreciate the deep love of all things Lance Bass, I was having a problem with the idea of forced giving to stay in the kingdom. Oh yeah, the kingdom wasn't just their term for the people who attended the church; the kingdom was heaven, and I was starting to surmise if you weren't bap-

kiersten lyons

tized into their kingdom, and their kingdom only, no pearly gates for you.

I arrived to Lisa's Bible study "to make up for the last one" at her spacious townhouse to find my closest friends inside, along with yummy brunch foods (yessssss). My plate piled high with treats, I noticed a *Cosmo* magazine and thumbed through, spotting Chris on one of the pages.

"Oh my gosh! This is the guy I was telling you about! The one I asked you guys to pray for. The one I had a big crush on in high school." *Also now, currently, but most of you don't know that because he's not in the kingdom.*

*I would like to take this time to apologize to you, Chris, you know, for asking a cult to pray for you and just generally telling them who you were....

We all got seated, paper plates filled with croissants as we thumbed through our Bibles for the first verse Lisa was mentioning, and that's when I noticed even though we were all in a circle, it seemed as if every chair was pointed towards me.

"Kiersten, what do you think about that?"

I hadn't even heard what she'd read, let alone what she'd asked. I was too busy noticing the seating situation. I asked if they could come back to me.

"Just take a look and see what you think?"

All eyes were on me now as Lisa read the verse again. It was about authority.

"Oh, okay—well, actually I think authority is really important, as long as it's humble and transparent."

crushed

At the word *transparent*, Lisa abruptly switched the subject. Another girl asked about a guy who had recently decided to become a pastor. I asked where he was going.

Lisa turned toward me. "What do you mean?"

"You know like for seminary, or divinity school—I'm not sure what it's called."

"He's learning under my husband."

"Oh, where'd your husband go?"

All the girls leaned in. Lisa narrowed her eyes at me as she began to switch subjects again, but she didn't need to, as someone else asked about specials. Were they supposed to be basing their percentage off their gross earning or their net? Lisa smiled, pleased with the question.

"Well, when you tell people how much you make, do you tell them your gross or your net? You tell your gross, don't you? That's how you should be treating this for God."

I raised my hand. "Where is it all going?"

"What?"

"Like the organization or charity. Any church I've ever been at, if there's an extra collection, it's always for a community in specific need."

The other girls leaned in, some nodding along, as Lisa's face grew increasingly tight.

"You don't have the authority to ask that question."

The whole room looked at me. A coldness set in. Gone was the warmth that had enveloped me for the past six weeks, now replaced with pointed questions. Lisa making sure I understood my place. She asked about me missing multiple

kiersten lyons

prayer services, the fact that I never took communion, and how dare I think I can question the elders.

How does she know I don't take their communion? I don't sit by her.

I tried to explain I didn't know what I believed about taking communion in other faiths since I was raised Catholic. I quoted the book of John, asking some questions about the church's beliefs, with the rest of the group flipping to John and looking it over too. They were leaning in, interested in my thoughts. Lisa's coldness turned to calculation, her eyes narrowing in like a predator on a nature documentary right before they pounce on their prey.

"Catholics aren't in the kingdom." Before I could respond she grabbed the *Cosmo* magazine from the coffee table, Chris's face now in her hands. "Kiersten's living in sin. She's lusting after this young man who is not in the kingdom. Kiersten is living in sin!"

Poor Chris, shirtless in a bed of hay, looked out from the page, his smoldering eyes crumpling as she waved the magazine this way and that. "I *know* you spent the night at this boy's house."

How does she know that?

She wasn't wrong—I did. But on his floor of his new place in Santa Monica because I was too tired to drive back to the valley. She didn't care. "Can you imagine what that looks like to other people that are outside of the kingdom? You are living in *sin*. You need to go to our rehab program. I've heard you got drunk in college."

She'd heard? How did she—?

crushed

I looked around the room, realizing my friends had been feeding her information.

"Your friends are concerned for your soul. They know you need the program, and they know your baptism wasn't valid. They love you and want you as part of the kingdom."

I was shaking at this point, much more than poor Chris on the now crumbled page. It all happened so fast. I tried to calmly explain I needed to talk to my parents about this and maybe even speak to a priest and hear his thoughts.

"Priests are agents of the devil." She then proceeded to tell me God brought me here to save my whole family and who knows who else, because Catholics are going to hell.

"You believe my parents are going to hell?"

Okay, so we're doing this.

I fired back that we can't judge someone's heart, and it concerned me she felt she had the authority to. I also was extremely concerned that the church was taking upwards of 40 percent of people's incomes with no accountability. In every church I'd ever attended, Catholic or otherwise, there is a transparent breakdown of all monies brought in and out. Where was the money going? There was no building to pay for, no maintenance to keep up. Who exactly did this money help? What were the pastors' salaries? Her newly built townhouse in one of the richest areas of the country seemed awfully nice. What about the fruit of the spirit? What about Jesus's whole poverty thing? And speaking of accountability, it was incredibly concerning that pastors were just taught from other pastors with no formal education or objective outside influence. Who was overseeing any of this? It seemed

kiersten lyons

she could just say what she wanted, and everyone listened with no ability to question.

"How *dare* you question me?" she spat.

"Isn't that what faith truly is?" I asked. "Asking questions? Trying to make sense of life?"

She was losing control of the room, and so she pulled her last card.

"Kiersten is not only lustful, not only prideful—she is refusing to submit to authority, and she is unteachable. Until you are ready to submit, ready to be taught, you are not welcomed back."

I swear there was a collective gasp, because she then said I was the first person ever in the LA chapter to be asked to leave. That's how evil I was.

Then she turned toward the girls. "You are more than welcome to stay friends with Kiersten, but just know it's your soul that will suffer." Or something equally poetic.

I left and went straight to Chris's. Within the hour I was there, legal notepad in hand, we drafted a document to sue them for defamation.

Just kidding. He was helping me write a song, one filled with angst and anger and all the other things twenty-one-year-olds feel after they've been kicked out of a cult for being "unteachable." Chris was the first person who ever called it a cult. He had called it that a week prior when I told him Lisa questioned my priorities when I missed a prayer service.

"Yeah…it's a cult."

crushed

He also fully believes he got me kicked out. "You were lusting after me, Kiersten," he reminds me, laughing all the way.

I refuse to let you have this one, Chris! My sharp questioning and general lack of "uh, you can't tell me my parents are going to hell" did it. But we did write one heck of a song about it—I mean, truly banger status (even though I don't remember one line or note of it).

And look, I don't know if you've ever been kicked out of a cult, but contrary to popular belief, it's not fun, and it's deeply painful. All at once I was back to square one in LA, except now I was unraveling the wasted time, and the times I was told over and over how I was going to hell.

It soon became a defining mark of how strong I was, a strengthening of muscles I would need to be able to let go of future heartbreaks, most especially allowing others to define my identity, my worth. There's no sitting on the *Tonight Show* couch for a cult, no "look at me now!" There's just the sober realization that the only way to soften the deepest piercings of rejection is to allow time to pass.

Years later, I came across an article where a woman recounted her eleven years in the same cult, their mind control and eventual coercion into her marrying a man they chose for her to continue the kingdom with. Every paragraph gave me chills, as if I was seeing my life in some alternative universe of what could've been. It was if my life was flashing before my eyes, completely overcome with the notion that rejection may, in fact, be the best thing that could ever happen to me, no matter how painful.

kiersten lyons

One day, years from now, when you least expect it, you'll have that confirmation too. Maybe a news article, maybe an email, maybe just a moment where your breath slows and for the first time in a long time you know you're going to be okay—but however it eventually comes, just know it will.

Rejection truly is protection.

But also, again, if you told me that during all of this, I would've smacked you—so please feel free to close this book and smack the shit out of it for a minute or two.

Chapter Fourteen

losing myself

I have some unsettling news, it's one that I'm honestly not even sure I'm ready to share, but I have promised you transparency, and so here I go:

Chris and I were not destined to be together.

I know, you're as shocked as I am. I mean, hello, we both moved three thousand miles from Montgomery County, Maryland, to a little town called Los Angeles, we were both funny, and he still had muscles; this was all the makings of great romance. And yet...

I don't know how to tell you the next part, but again: honesty. Sometimes when we actually get to hang out with our crush (read: obsession), we find out that we're not even remotely romantically compatible. Like, if you dated each other, you would, in fact, murder each other. Don't get me wrong, Chris and I loved each other, but like, in a brother-sister way, and that truly shocked me to my core.

Me? Wrong about boys? No!

Chris became my big brother in LA. He'd been there six months longer than me, and anytime I would complain

kiersten lyons

about something, from the fake conversations to the insane traffic to the mean casting directors, he'd look at his wrist with no watch on it and go, "Hmm, a year here? Yeah, you're right on time."

I pivoted quick from two months of life devoted to a cult to a life devoted back to my career—a career filled with mailing headshots and resumes, doing background work to try to learn the ropes of being on set and having an acting coach I spent so much money on tell me to grow my eyebrows out "because your face isn't symmetrical, and it may help."

Non-symmetrical face or not, I had been asked to be a regular extra on the final season of NBC's *Just Shoot Me* starring David Spade, and after months of doing background work and being treated like a literal piece of the background, this was way better. Every Friday the audience would arrive, and for a couple of hours I'd get to watch the lead actors and hilarious guest stars work, from last minute ad libs to mid-scene dance parties. I was the youngest on set and took it as a masterclass in all things sitcom. Plus, I made the cast laugh on multiple occasions, even the director once or twice, but I always knew my place—an extra never talks to the actors unless spoken to first. It was like how children were treated in the 1930s, only with craft services!

The night the cast took their final bow; I teared up, sad for them but happy tears for me. I just knew my turn was coming soon.

My own sitcom at twenty-four, married at twenty-five, and my first baby by twenty-six. A most perfect MASH!

crushed

My whole life was planned out; I even passed off working with a music producer my landlord had set me up with because "I know exactly what I want and can't let anything derail it."

After the cult debacle, it was as if I had blinders on, focused on my own sitcom, which meant anything left over after bills (most months, nothing) was spent on an agent workshop, makeup, or more headshots. I thought by now I'd be going on those dozens of auditions a month (like E! told me I would—besides, Chris was!) but instead I was trying to get just one agent or manager to meet with me. Apparently winning Best Actor in fifth grade or multiple Thespian awards in high school weren't what they were looking for.

There had been one moment of breakthrough—a kid I used to coach on the swim team had a much older half-brother who was a commercial director in LA. He was directing a film, and somehow my dad found out and pitched me to his dad, and three thousand miles from LA, on the pool deck of Waters Landing Pool A (not B, where I almost died from dehydration), I somehow got an audition, with the director telling his dad, "Look, I'll bring her in, but she has to audition like everybody else. I've got legit actors in this; I'm not just giving her the role because you know her dad."

This is where you find out, yes, I am a nepo baby, because I booked that shiz! (And by shiz, I mean an unpaid short film.)

But it was three days of being on set, three days of getting my hair and makeup done, of sitting in video village, of being treated like an equal and being gushed over by the director, producers, and other cast members.

kiersten lyons

IT WAS GLORIOUS.

But we were now eight months later, and I was so tired of pounding the pavement, so when a fellow background actor on *Just Shoot Me* told me a bunch of his friends were hanging out that night, and I should come, I said, "Yeah, I should!" A cold beer (okay, wine cooler) sounded lovely.

I got to the place we were meeting at—an apartment in Park LaBrea, the quintessential LA apartment complex, where everyone knows at least someone who had lived there, will live there, or is currently living there. I think I was one of two girls—mostly guys, all former frat boys from Kentucky, some trying to be actors, some producers. I liked them all right away. We grabbed some cabs and headed out to the Sunset Strip to grab drinks. I was so focused on my career I wasn't even looking at any of the boys with anything other than friendship, until one boy stopped looking at me. We'll call him Brian. He was growing increasingly distant throughout the night. Anytime I asked him anything, he would answer with a shrug and move away. It was becoming apparent he was ignoring me.

And what do we do with boys who ignore us?

That's right! Become increasingly attracted to them!

By the end of the second time we all hung out, I was completely smitten, because he was completely not giving me the time of day! I soon learned he was ignoring me was because his friend who had invited me out in the first place

crushed

liked me, but Brian was starting to have feelings all while trying to be a good friend. Okay, so yeah, basically I'm smack dab in the middle of *The Summer I Turned Pretty* (you know twenty years before it came out), and *I was loving it.*

I mean, if Jesus was my faith, then romcoms were my religion. It wasn't just *Grease* that informed my romantic ideals but the entire genre (musical numbers not needed but always appreciated).

From *When Harry Met Sally* to *Ten Things I Hate About You* (and every makeover scene in between), I was steeped in the time-honored tradition of not only the boys finally realizing their true feelings, but also changing...for you. I mean, have you seen season three of *Bridgerton*?!

Because that's how you know when it's true love—when they change...FOR YOU.

And I know Julia Roberts got the big hat and gloves and stopped being a prostitute, thus seeming like she was the changed one, but alas, that is false. She still was very much herself (Arsenio Hall–style cheering at the polo match and all) because in the end, what good ol' Richard Gere offered wasn't good enough for her.

She walked out. Richard Gere was the one realizing his asshole ways—he changed his business practices, he climbed the fire escape even though he was scared, and he ran after her because he realized how incredible she truly she was.

Ahhh, true love.

Brian asked me to see *How to Lose a Guy in 10 Days* but not tell his friend yet; we should see if there was anything between us. Spoiler Alert: there very much was. He was funny and sweet, so I got super scared. Did he want a shy girl like high school Chris? Did he want a girl who was weak and couldn't push him over like first-grade Matty? Did he want a girl who would sleep with him like every other guy?

No, no, Kiersten, remember: real love is when a guy changes...FOR YOU.

I went into my first real relationship with this tucked squarely into my subconscious as we kept hanging out, kept making out, and I kept waiting for the moment he'd realize it was okay we weren't having sex because I was worth it. One night while we were making out, I got a sudden burst of clarity, mixed with a confident confusion of sorts. I knew I loved him; I knew I wanted to marry him, but I knew my heart needed, well...

"Who's your best friend?"

"Uh...Gavin. Why, who's yours?"

He leaned back in to kiss me, smiling at how flustered I was, you know, because romcom girls are always adorably flustered.

"Mine's Jesus. Jesus is my best friend. I need Jesus to be your best friend too!"

"Well, I'm Jewish, so..."

I was no longer adorable; I was annoying. Why couldn't I just be normal, he asked? A normal girl in a normal relationship having normal sex? Why did God have to come into it?

We were at an impasse, both of us wanting to be together, but what that together meant was so different. I teared up, and then he did too. Our relationship literally started with

crushed

Kate Hudson trying to lose a guy, and here I was fully succeeding in the mission.

I can't do this again. I'm so sick of being alone, rejected, crushed. I mean, loud girls are supposed to be slutty, and praying girls are supposed to quiet. Nobody likes the loud girl who prays!

So, I stopped praying. I stopped being funny and even stopped being loud, because I wanted so badly to be normal. I wanted so badly to be what he wanted, because I didn't want to lose him.

But when you cling so tight to keep something, you end up losing yourself.

"I'm sick of wearing condoms, and we can't get pregnant."

I had been on the pill briefly in college, for my random cycles.

Yes, doctor, it's about my irregular cycles and not all because I want boobs!

I hated how I felt on it, emotionally and physically, so within a few months of going on, I went right off. But now Brian said we needed it, and I needed him, so I got back on, and the boobs came back. Which was a delight for Brian, as he had a huge thing for Jessica Simpson (it was 2003—every guy did), so alongside my newfound chest, I also added highlights and big hoop earrings. Brian didn't specifically ask me to do any of this. It was more that I saw how much he loved

kiersten lyons

that look, so I became it. I stopped going to church and even started to be late to auditions.

During this time, I also got a talent manager, a truly sweet story that involved meeting a casting assistant, Sara. I was now a stylist at an expensive store at the Beverly Center, and she was there trying to find an outfit for an Emmys event. I watched her face as she tried on top after top, her smile fading, and I knew that face so well.

The "I don't like myself in this outfit…I will never be good enough" face.

I offered to take her to another store on my break, because I didn't want anyone to feel what I felt so many times over. I hadn't prayed much lately, or at all, but something told me to.

"I may sound like a weirdo, but I'm going to pray you find something you feel beautiful in."

She laughed, telling me I was different than other actresses. Those words felt different this time; I wasn't trying prove anything—I just was being me. I found her a top at Bloomingdale's, and she found me a manager (who was in Burbank—see, it is where fancy people are!), and I began going on my first real auditions. Well, sort of…

Most casting directors told my manager they didn't know what to do with me.

"She's so talented, but we really don't have anything for her look."

But then one did—a huge guest star spot I was perfect for. It was my role to lose. But I was too busy losing myself to Brian and never really worked on it. Read it over a few times

crushed

but went in completely unprepared. I didn't bomb, but was just fine, and I walked out knowing I'd completely thrown away my shot.

Brian and I were fighting a lot, sometimes about real stuff (I hated that we all partied so much and were always with all his friends) but oftentimes we would just fight because twenty-two-year-olds are not the best at communication. I mean, I was always right, and even if I wasn't, I had given him my virginity, and that was huge, and so deep down I think I always held that card in our fights.

Healthy, I know.

I was holding so much in, the toll of not being myself was getting to me, and I was starting to forget who I was. We had talked so much about the future, about marriage, but I was exhausted thinking about going on like this. And so, I did the most logical thing in the world; I called my big brother.

Because that guy can be trusted with my feelings.

Except he could. Because right before I moved to LA, Luke had apologized for everything. For how much he tormented me and for his being cruel our entire childhood (although sometimes singing Broadway show tunes at the top of one's lungs over and over can be annoying—I'll give him that). He told me how proud he was of me for going to LA, for pursuing my dreams, and now as I cried to him over the phone, he asked me some questions. Was I happy? Had I forgotten my dreams? Myself? Is this the kind of relationship I actually wanted?

kiersten lyons

Oh, because you just got married, you're now some relationship guru.

Sarcasm aside, he wasn't wrong, and a few days before my birthday, I broke it off. Or as someone I worked with said, "Wow, you really are a good person. Who breaks up with someone before their birthday? At least get your present first."

I was a *wreck*, and not just because it was the saddest birthday I had ever known (and when you have a big brother who thinks it's funny to chase you around the house with the cake knife, you've known some pretty sad birthdays…I know, I know, he apologized, and I did forgive him, but chasing your sister with a knife kind of leaves a lasting mark, people!).

Months before, in an attempt to save the relationship, I moved from Burbank to Hollywood to be closer to Brian, but now it just meant I would have more chances to run into him. This is what I was sobbing to my parents as they casually bought me a plane ticket home. "We miss you," they'd said, which really meant, "You are not emotionally in a place to be alone."

They weren't wrong. Chris was taking me to the airport, but not before a little birthday brunch. A month prior he had gone through a breakup and knew this heartache well. We were sitting at a little place on Melrose when I saw a knit poncho (leave me alone—they were all the rage in 2004) in the shop's window next door and began crying. Brian had always told me they looked stupid, and so I never got one.

"I loved him so much. I miss him so much. I hurt him so much."

crushed

Like the good big brother he was becoming, Chris encouraged me to go try it on. To be fair, I think he also didn't know how to handle my public tears or the fact I was such a ball of confusion.

I tucked that poncho in my bag, not ready to wear it, not ready to admit Brian and I were truly over.

February in Maryland is sad and grey, sometimes icy, and always barren—it was perfect for a girl grieving her first real love. I was so sure I would spend every waking moment on my parents' couch bawling my eyes out, but my sisters had other plans. And by plans, I mean to stay up late and tell me all their best high school freshman stories until we all were laughing so hard we almost peed our pants.

I realized how much I missed the day-to-day of being a big sister, one moment offering advice, the next fighting over the last bite of a Wendy's Frosty. After a year of completely losing myself, in just a few short days I was finding me again, and Hallie and Annie had everything to do with it. Hallie was witty, sharp, and did everything she possibly could to not grow up. Annie had that same wit but coupled it with a need to know everything and very much wanting to grow up right now. They would wake me up each morning fighting about something ridiculous as they got ready for school, and I loved every minute of it.

But it wasn't just them. Most days that I was back home, we added Cori to the mix. Cori and I had met right before I had moved to LA, when I was directing a smashing comedy retelling of *The Nativity Story* for her and other high school

kiersten lyons

students at a local church that met at my high school (which I guess made the whole cult meeting at a nightclub less weird).

And if you're all, "The nativity story isn't funny," well, Cori played the angel Gabriel who had a Bluetooth earpiece with a direct line to God, so obviously now you know you're wrong.

Cori soon became my third little sister, and anytime I was home, the four of us would try do our best to come up with the most ridiculous outfits from my sisters' childhood dress ups and then have a photo shoot until, yes, we almost peed in our pants (a theme in our sisterhood).

I didn't want to go back to LA; I wanted to stay in the safety of my childhood home forever, but I had rent and auditions and that whole "most likely to become famous" bit, so I flew back, but not without filling out an application first.

I had first looked into becoming a Big Sister through Big Brothers Big Sisters right before I started dating Brian, but then I did the whole, "completely lose myself for a guy and forget about anything that doesn't include him" thing and never finished the application. But now, as my sisters, Cori, and I all hugged so tightly outside the airport (me sporting the poncho), I knew it was such a testament to who I really was, to who I was created to be.

Plus, I'd finally have someone to watch Disney movies with!

That was something Brian would always comment about—how much I loved Disney. He thought it was babyish, and why couldn't I be like normal girls who liked *The Breakfast Club*? This was his measure of maturity, and I went

crushed

right along with it, my love of Disney being mostly put on the back burner.

My interview process was longer than most, Sandra, my caseworker, said. Right away, my background of working with kids meant I had been thought of for a few different programs within the organization, and upon my final interview Sandra said, "I know exactly who I am going to match you with."

In July 2005, I was matched with my Little Sister, Ashley.

Chapter Fifteen ♡

california dreaming

Los Angeles was slowly starting to become home, again with Chris looking at his wrist with the nonexistent watch and saying, "Two years? Yeah, that's about right."

And at three years, I finally booked my first guest star.

I sat at the table read for TNT's *The Closer* so nervous to make eye contact with anyone because I was so used to the rules of background work—don't make eye contact, don't speak unless spoken to (basically, you're a tree). The guy who was playing my boyfriend had been a lead on *Dawson's Creek*, and I was sure at any minute he and everyone else would know my only professional experience was background work and yell for me to leave the table at once.

But something altogether different happened: they all welcomed me with open arms, most especially Kyra Sedgewick, who I didn't have any scenes with but was so kind at the table read and made sure to ask me all about myself. It was intoxicating to be treated like I mattered.

Wait, do I matter?

crushed

I didn't have time to ponder that much because it was back to my weeks filled with working whatever job at the moment to pay the bills—and there were a lot of them. While trying to pay rent as a struggling actress, you already know I worked retail, tray passed at private events, and nannied, but I also was a hostess, server, cocktail waitress, swim lessons instructor, stylist for the host on a bridal reality TV show, a personal assistant, a birthday party princess for five years (why, yes, I was the one who created the Hannah Montana full theme birthday party complete with a full choreographed show for the birthday girl and her besties to learn and perform, thank you for asking) and perhaps the best job? Like ever, of all time? In the history of struggling actors?

One Black Friday weekend I walked around a random mall deep in the Valley with a large GAP bag stuffed with brown paper and a puffy vest on top. I would go into competing stores and say loudly to my friend (a.k.a., the girl I just met), "Oh, this top is cute, but at GAP they're having buy one get one half off, so I think we should head back there…"

And then we'd leave to perform this drama in another unsuspecting store for eight hours straight. I know what you're thinking; yes, this is marketing at its finest.

I'd usually hope for a commercial audition a week, maybe if I was lucky a TV guest spot audition every month, and I worked six days a week to pay bills (saving Fridays for Ashley and our ice cream sundaes). I would scoop her up after school, sometimes right outside of it, and we would pop in a CD and sing at the top of our lungs as we sat in Friday LA traffic. Her favorites were Alicia Keys and Kanye's *The College Dropout*;

kiersten lyons

she would do the crazy inhales on Kayne's "Jesus Walks," and every time I would fall for it, whipping my head around, sure she was having a seizure. She would laugh so loud.

"Kiki, you should see your face! Every single time!"

It would drive me crazy, but I didn't care; seeing her sing along to everything from Ariel to Alicia Keys made the long drives worth it. Plus, Brian and I were in the middle of the inevitable "maybe we should get back together" dance that lasted on and off for three years, and I was in the middle of the mid-twenties "who am I, and what do I want?" crisis.

I take that back—I knew exactly what I wanted, and *nothing* was coming true. I was about to be twenty-six and had no TV show, no husband, and was very much not pregnant. My perfect MASH wasn't even close, and I was so…old.

Twenty-six is at least fifty-seven in Hollywood years, and I was running out of time (and collagen in my face). One night, while out with Chris and our best friends Rand and Kristen, a friend called to tell me all about her engagement. My face registered death, and naturally, all three were concerned.

"Kiersten, what happened?"

"Katie is engaged."

Chris and Rand made gag faces. They were extremely good-looking guys with symmetrical faces in their twenties; the idea of marriage or even kind of tying oneself down was at best perplexing, but more like certain death. Kristen understood a bit more and wrapped me up in a hug as I whispered, "My life is slipping away, and I have nothing to show

crushed

for it," or something equally as level-headed. She squeezed my shoulders, reminding me it would be okay.

But would it? Could it?

All three of them were what the industry decided was hot, all three of them got multiple auditions a week, Chris had been a lead on *The OC* for goodness' sakes, and I could barely get a legit audition a month—and even then, it was usually two lines as an awkward assistant or future dead body on *Cold Case*.

Forget thousands or even hundreds of auditions like E! promised me; I was five years in and hadn't even hit forty-five. Doors closing was one thing, but most months I couldn't even get near a door, let alone watch it close. And the few times I did? The few times the pipeline worked, where my headshot was deemed "attractive enough," casting deemed me "the right look" for producers, I almost always booked.

I would walk in the room, sometimes crawling with a director and producers, and immediately make them laugh, immediately turn the small little part into something bigger with the eventual, "Why haven't we met you before?"

I hated that question, because I wanted to scream, "Because none of you will give me a chance!" But instead, I'd just smile. That's exactly how I booked *The Closer* and a few other TV shows, and my manager had started getting feedback on how funny I was. Which was fantastic because apparently comedy shows and movies didn't need the small noses and big teeth that dramas did, and so she started submitting me more for them—except they wanted assurance that I was

kiersten lyons

funny before I got in the room. They needed to see where I was "studying."

Apparently, being bullied mercilessly as a kid to make you funny wasn't a good enough school, so just days before my dreaded twenty-sixth birthday, I enrolled in classes at The Groundlings, a highly sought after improv school in LA. Think Will Ferrell, Melissa McCarthy, and Kristen Wiig.

Why the hell are we only now seeing I should be in comedy? Why didn't I start classes here so much earlier? Such wasted time!

But when you meet your manager in the middle of a relationship where you've lost yourself, how the hell would she know how funny you were if you forgot it too?

I loved and hated that class; it stretched me, often making me question if I was even funny. It also opened me up to real comedy: the truth of it all. I had an acting teacher in college say, "Whatever you're working on, on the stage, as an actor, you're working on in real life, too," and this class was stabbing with that notion. I was starting to learn I didn't have to try—I just had to be.

The class was filled with people in their early to mid-twenties, some funny, some extremely funny. There was one guy, Bradley, who arrived one day in a Young Life t-shirt (which is Christian ministry for high school students). I was intrigued, but also not. I had met some funny guys who liked God in college, but they never liked the funny girl—always the quiet ones (let's not forget, nobody likes the loud girl who prays)—plus I was sure his shirt was just an ironic thrift store find. That same day I came with ashes on my forehead because it

crushed

was Ash Wednesday, and someone tried to be kind by telling me I had dirt on my face.

"Nah, I just love me some Jesus."

The whole class laughed, and I realized maybe just being me was okay. Over time I fell into the rhythm, learning that listening and "yes, and-ing" was way funnier than trying to think of a joke. In comedy, the more you try to prove yourself, the less you are successful.

Huh...

During one class, our incredible teacher had Bradley and I go up onstage. From the minute the scene started, it was just easy, our back and forth, and then Bradley threw out a line about the 1990s Disney movie *Operation Dumbo Drop*.

Okay, but who is this guy?

He ended up having to leave class because of a work thing and messaged me on MySpace (yes, I said MySpace—it was 2007, and MySpace was *also* everything, leave me alone!) and while driving home from my friend's bridal shower, we talked. For an hour and a half. He made me laugh so hard, actually did love God (he thought my line about Jesus was funny), and we couldn't stop talking (so much so my phone died, and I had to plug it up in a Walmart bathroom). I immediately called my best friend, Amy.

"I think I'm going to marry this guy."

We went out to lunch a few days later, and I was so excited, like, could this be...?

NEVERMIND.

He was just so nice. Where's the spark in nice? Plus, he listened to me. I didn't have to try to get him to. Where's the

kiersten lyons

push and pull in that? The butterflies? I tried so hard but felt nothing. I really thought it would be something, and I ended up more devastated than before. So, I did the most mature thing a girl could do: I ghosted him.

Don't worry, I soon met another guy, Parker, who was funny and mentioned God when we talked, but he also kind of ignored me, so…JACKPOT!

We soon started seeing each other, him laughing at my jokes and even seeming to appreciate my whole "not having sex" thing. Things were going so well that I casually tried on glass rings at Forever21 just to see how they looked. I was sure he'd ask me to be exclusive when instead, he told me he had tried to like me, tried to be attracted to me, but just couldn't, but then kept asking if I wanted to hang out.

I know what you're thinking, and you would be right: this poor guy just didn't realize he loved me yet. He was like my old rugby partner Matty! One night he asked me if I wanted to go on a drive down to the OC to see where he dreamed of buying a house and raising a family?

Uh, well I'm kind of in love and want to marry you, so… "YES!"

We walked along the sand as the moon danced on the water, his hand reaching for mine as he showed me the house he wanted to buy one day. I was so sure that this was the moment he'd tell me he was in love with me. We climbed back into his truck to head back, passing a little elementary school as he said, "And that's where Kallie will teach kindergarten."

crushed

Kallie? You mean your former high school girlfriend, Kallie?!? But your fingers are intertwined with mine! YOU'RE DOING THE THUMB RUB!

The thumb rub is so much more than holding hands. It says, "I like you so much I'm going to exert a bit of energy with my thumb!"

I wish I could tell you I pulled my hand away, but I didn't. I just sat on the drive back so humiliated, confused, crushed.

Parker wants a teacher? But I gave up teaching in kindergarten because I was so sure Kevin wanted an actress. Do I go back and tell my childhood dolls that I am going back to teaching because Parker wants a—

No. NO!

I can't do this anymore. I'm so tired of changing myself for guys. For casting directors. For cults! And no matter what, I am never enough.

I told Parker I couldn't hang out anymore, and I didn't just say it but actually followed through. No more "twisting myself up like a pretzel" (my mom's words) to get someone to like me. So much so that when I went out with an incredibly handsome actor from one of my favorite TV shows, I refused to be anybody but me, and he liked it…until he didn't. Because he soon realized, heartthrob status or not, I wasn't staying over, and it made him so mad. I found the whole thing hilarious as the boy had not even tried to hold my hand yet and somehow, he was so put out by the fact I wouldn't put out. Seriously, when I told him I was going to head home the night of our third date, he went from being the kindest guy to not even walking me to my car—on the street in the

kiersten lyons

pitch black. He just stood on his porch so frustrated I hadn't succumbed to his charm.

I began to write all these revelations and stories down, and not just in journals. I had realized in Groundlings how much I loved satire and had been doing it naturally ever since that pretend love note to Ivan. Except I had thankfully learned satire (and all the best comedy in general) wasn't to take down the weak—that was cruel. No, it was to question the powerful, to poke holes, and what started out as funny little posts on MySpace turned into full sketches. I was writing sketches about dating, about Hollywood, about trying to fit in, about celebrities, and they were good.

David Spade even came back into my life. I met one of his producers on a short-lived show that mocked Hollywood news a la E! Entertainment. I send the producer some of my stuff, and he liked it. The show was cancelled before I even got a meeting, but it didn't matter—I was hooked. Being an actor and saying other people's lines was great, but writing your own stuff? Oh, that's way better.

If my life was a romcom, then this was the scene in *Runaway Bride* where Julia Roberts is trying to figure out what eggs she likes, and apparently the eggs I liked were filled with wit and laughter and heart. I was equally confident about and annoyed with Hollywood now, almost as if I didn't care (but don't worry, I still did, A LOT).

Which is how I walked into Bar Marmont that night to celebrate Sage's birthday. That night I met James. Annoyed at the scene, as everyone trying to be seen, yet equally finding humor in all of it. For the first time ever, I wasn't trying to be

crushed

anything but me, and the guy behind the bar was intrigued. I made him laugh, I never shied away from my intelligence, and I was confident in my faith and what I wanted.

The guy who could have had anyone wanted me. He chose me. All of me.

I was enough. I was finally enough....

part three

"THE BREAKTHROUGH"

CUE: "LOSE YOU TO LOVE ME," SELENA GOMEZ

Chapter Sixteen

enough

I looked at my phone. My message had just sent, and the three dots of uncertainty had already appeared. I say uncertain because just as quickly as they can appear, they often vanish. (Not to be confused with the Fox show *Vanished* I worked on for three episodes I was sure would be my big break, until it vanished off the air.) And when the dots do disappear, we're left with the knowledge that the other person read it, almost replied, and then didn't.

But they will later, right?

You check your phone, you make sure the ringer is up, then decide, no, it's best to go on silent. You lock your phone and turn it over, trying to walk away. But as quickly as you put it down, you lift it right back up, sure the response will be there.

This dance is the worst, (but also kind of the best) because it's filled with highs and lows and butterflies. Something tells me you get it. No, no like...**YOU GET IT**.

One thing I discovered from that last call to James (you remember, the call where I begged him to sleep with me

kiersten lyons

months after he had literally thrown me away like a piece of trash), and what I wish everyone who's going through a terrible heartbreak, whether it's by a boy or a dream or a freaking cult, knew:

You are going to want to call them after you swore you never would.

People will tell you just to block them. "It's that easy," they'll say. And that's some bullshit. Because I did. I followed all the best advice; immediately after he called off the wedding, I toggled that stupid 917 number to block. His family, too. Not out of spite, but pain, and boy did I feel strong the minute I did it. I was the heartbreak champion!

Until I wasn't. Because guess what?

You will want to call them after you swore you wouldn't.

For a myriad of reasons. Maybe you think you need more closure; maybe you feel you didn't properly tell them how badly they hurt you, and if you could just explain it a different way, then they would finally understand. Or maybe it's the date you were supposed to fly to New York for your wedding, and how could he tell you he would love you for forever and then throw you away like a piece of trash?!

Either way, no matter how hard you toggle that button to block, you can just toggle that shit right back. It's just that easy. Which is where I found myself the night at camp when I blew up his phone over and over and over again. I just couldn't resist.

And in all my years of sitting beside those in the middle of deep heartbreak, I've only met one person who was able to

crushed

fully block—and it was her old job. *One* person, and it was a *job*. Now's not the time for you to try to be the second. It's okay to not be strong, and it's okay to be cuddled up under a blanket and delete their number like someone at camp suggested.

So that's what I did next. It worked for a bit, but you know that drill...

Because in those moments when reality takes a break, when the truth is muddled and all you can remember is the good stuff, when you can't get to this book fast enough to see your moments of clarity, when you refuse to open the notes app on your phone to remind you of the truth...in those moments it doesn't matter if their contact is gone from your phone, because you know it by heart. You'll just type that sucker in.

One. Number. At. A. Time.

And even though you've promised everyone you'll never contact him again—your family, your friends, yourself—you are. So don't delete his number.

DELETE HIS NAME.

Give him a new one. One that will shock your senses back to reality, one that no matter how hard you try, reminds you of the truth, that gives you a visual and won't let you go, because he *did* let you go.

On Thanksgiving of 2009, six months after James first called off our wedding, golf superstar Tiger Woods called off his marriage. I mean, technically his wife was the one who filed for divorce, but his years of cheating on her solidified his position on commitment. Not so solidified was his car's windshield, which, upon learning of his continued infidelity, his wife smashed with his prized golf clubs.

The minute I saw that news, I changed James's name in my phone.

And it worked. Oh boy, did it work, because just days after changing it, James won a freaking reality show with a giant cash prize. That's right—while your girl was struggling to pay rent, her ex (who cheated *and* already had a trust fund) won $100,000!

A HUNDRED THOUSAND DOLLARS.

I felt the urge to text him, not sure what I would even say, except for all I had just screamed at God.

"I was the only one who believed in him, the only one who ever stuck around, who ever truly loved him, and he left me like I never mattered—and now he wins the equivalent of a down payment on a house in the Hollywood Hills, and I'm barely able to pay my cell phone bill?! He turned his back on you, God. I'm all, "Thy will be done!" and You give him a $100,000?! This is the worst. He is the worst. You are the worst! He is a winner, and I'm still a…what did my brother always call me? A loser! I'm a loser!"

Why is life so unfair?!

I furiously typed in his number, but before I could write one word of my incredible monologue, one word of all the injustice that was my life, James's new name had appeared.

Tiger Woods.

crushed

Suddenly, I saw myself years down the road, smashing James's windshield—not with a golf club, but with a stupid cocktail shaker.

I immediately stopped texting. Peace surrounded me.

That stupid, freaking peace.

In that moment, I knew this pain, as horrible as it was, was better than *that* pain... And if I listened to this pain— if, like a fever, I let it do its job, I would never have to go through that *worse* pain.

I could finally be free.

Chapter Seventeen

lowering the red flag

I couldn't stay at Sage's any longer. She was one of my closest friends, but her place was not even a block from James's. He wasn't there anymore (I can't remember how I knew that), but it didn't matter—that balcony was, and every night as I circled the block looking for parking, I was right back where I started, right back on that balcony being told I was that I wasn't enough.

And that's when hand-holding, thumb-rubbing Parker came back. He felt terrible about the way he had treated me years before and when he found out what James did and that I was looking for a place, he offered to let me crash with him. His roommate was at his girlfriend's all the time, and Parker had an extra bed. Literally, a bed—he lived in a studio apartment with two double beds in the main room. I jumped at the chance to be away from that balcony, and within twenty-four hours I had moved my little bits of stuff (everything else was still in storage) to Parker's place.

Parker was the first person who knew the whole story without ever knowing James, and with almost everything

crushed

I shared, big or small, Parker would just look at me, put a finger up, and say, "Red flag."

No matter how many times I tried to defend James, Parker would gently note, "Kiersten, I had a messed-up childhood too. It didn't give me the right to treat you the way I did."

My dad was trying to help me sell the ring, but he needed the documents that were in storage. Anytime I even thought about that storage pod, my chest tightened. James and I had packed much of it up together, the same day that divorced dad picked up my mattress. As James and I were playing a real-life game of Tetris, trying to stuff my sofa, dresser, and my whole life into like seven by nine feet, he looked up at me with the sweetest face and said something like, "The next time we unlock this, it'll be at our own place."

Liar.

But now that metal pod just sat somewhere in the valley collecting dust. Made clear by the tiny forklift driving it towards me and all of it billowing out all around only made worse when it was unceremoniously dropped in the dirt patch right in front of me.

I can't do this.

Parker assured me I could. I tried to take a breath, but with my tightened chest and the dirt still swirling around us, all I did was sputter out a cough, which made Parker and I both laugh. I grabbed the lock and together we pushed up the gate, hot air rushing out and memories rushing in. It was like a time capsule pointing to a girl who was so unaware. I tried to take another breath, thinking the air could stop the stinging realization, but all I got was the hot air.

kiersten lyons

All I ever got was hot air...

I quickly grabbed the box with the documents, forgetting it didn't just hold the papers, but our whole relationship. Every card and note, the receipt from our engagement dinner, the napkin I first wrote my number on, and so many pictures, our engagement ones on top.

We had this idea to go to JCPenney in the ugliest sweaters we could find and take early '90s photos. We stayed in character the entire time, laughing as the photographer didn't know what to make of us. It was one of my favorite things about us, how much we made each other laugh. I stared at the box, knowing what I needed to do, but frozen in fear. Parker offered to throw it in the dumpster for me, but I knew I had to be the one to do it. So instead, he offered his hand.

Our fingers weren't intertwined this time, and he most definitely was *not* doing the thumb rub, just gently squeezing my hand as I said goodbye to an entire two years of my past, and to everything I was so sure would be my future.

Parker held my hand for that entire next month, both physically and metaphorically, as I started to realize that heartbreak could be redeemed, and I was going to be okay. So okay, in fact, I was moving out. I found a little apartment just a few blocks from where Brian had lived when we broke up. The location was soothing, a gentle reminder that "this too shall pass." But I didn't have time to really dwell on that, because a cute boy was driving past me as I was taking my last box out of Parker's place.

That guy's cute.... Wait, I know that guy!

crushed

I had randomly thought about him just a few days before as I was driving home from an audition. *I wonder what that Bradley guy is up to. I bet he's married with a kid or something; he was such a nice guy.*

It probably had something to do with the fact that the day before, while I was at lunch with Chris, Parker walked by, and I had finally introduced the two. My eyes volleyed back and forth, growing wider as they shook hands, because I was shook. I mean, here were two of the biggest crushes of my life, boys I had cried buckets over, who were now like brothers to me.

So, I called Bradley. I mean, yes, he was cute, but really, I was just looking for people to hang out with who had nothing to do with James, and there's nothing that says "nothing to do with James" like being "too nice." But it wasn't currently calling, because currently my phone was screeching in my ear as a loud, angry sound let me know the person I was trying to reach had changed their number. I shrugged, trying to let it go, but something told me to keep trying, and so I did what any internet sleuth would do: I called my mommy.

Internet wasn't set up at my new place, I didn't have an iPhone yet (give me a little credit—it was still 2009), and my sisters were in class. My mom who'd just learned to double click a mouse—not an exaggeration—ever so carefully (i.e., SLOWLY) read through my Facebook friends list.

"I don't see a Bradley here, sweetie."

So, I painstakingly spelled out my MySpace password to her multiple times—"No, Mom, it's a capital L, then a lowercase o. Yes, capital L—" until she finally got in and I finally

kiersten lyons

learned his last name so we could go back over to Facebook and message him. I transcribed a super breezy message for my mom to type out, and within a couple of hours Bradley texted me, but not before my mom called once more.

"Sweetie, Bradley is very funny. He has some of his stand-up bits on the MySpace place you took me to, and he is just so funny. And clean too. No cursing."

My mom was right; he was funny, and the kid didn't curse. Within minutes, Bradley and I were bantering back and forth via text until he called me.

HE JUST PICKED UP A PHONE AND CALLED ME!

We learned that my new apartment was literal blocks from his place (an insane coincidence in a city with ten million people, where driving two miles can take forty-five minutes in traffic).

We spent the next month repeating this pattern: constant bantering and talking, oftentimes in person and until late at night. It was pretty clear there was something there, and it was also clear I was so unbelievably scared about it. So, we just hung out, making each other laugh, and occasionally me trauma dumping the last year on him.

We had gotten to the place where nothing was off limits, which meant me looking at him one night and going, "So is there anything you'd like to talk about? Anything at all? Anything you think we should talk about? Like maybe something you would like to say to me...about me?"

I opened that door real wide.

He laughed, looking at me with such equal conviction and wholesomeness, "I think it's pretty fair to say I like you.

crushed

A lot. But I also know you just got out of something huge, so I want to take it slow. I want to make sure you're okay."

Well, this is new.

There were moments when I was so sure he would kiss me, so sure he'd *do something*, but he was true to his word and ever so carefully we got closer. Until one Sunday afternoon I got a text while I was nannying for the family. I immediately cornered the kids' mom, Emmy, who was grabbing a snack in their pantry. I shoved my phone over to her, my hands shaking as she studied it.

"He asked what I was doing next week? We just usually hang out; he never asks me so far in advance."

Emmy looked back at his text, smiling,

"He's gonna ask you out on a proper date."

I knew she was right, but I was so scared. I looked around at the pantry; it was like the ones you see on *The Home Edit*. Everything perfectly in its place, organized, and with those handwritten labels. Nothing about my life at the moment was in its place or organized, and I definitely wasn't ready for labels.

When he asked me out (Emmy was spot on—he even said, "I'd like to take you on a real date"), he asked if there was a specific type of food I'd want.

How does one say they don't want any food for dinner?

I know I like a guy when I can't eat around him. Not because I'm nervous for him to see me consume food, but

kiersten lyons

rather the nerves make my stomach turn to stone, and the thought of food makes me ill.

"Anywhere with soup."

He gave me the cutest confused look but assured me he'd find a place.

When he picked me up, he was holding a red gerbera daisy; it was sweet, but something in me sank. I don't like red, and gerbera daisies aren't my favorite. Was this just like our lunch years before? When I wanted something to be there that just wasn't?

I tried to remind myself it was just the first date and thanked him for the little flower as I climbed into his 2001 Ford Focus hatchback that was very much not a brand-new Audi. But then again, Bradley was very much not James.

James once wanted to get me sunglasses; apparently my four-dollar Forever 21 glasses weren't up to his standards, so he took me to get Ray-Bans. I fell in love with the avia-tors—they felt good on my face, hiding my nose I was still so insecure about, but even more than that, I felt like me in them. James wanted me to wear the original Wayfarer ones. They were the choice around town and among his trust-fund friends (although for them these were their throw-around pair.)

We went back and forth, me (and the entire store) liking my choice, him pushing for the hipster ones. A few weeks later, for Valentine's Day, he presented me with Ray-Bans, snuck in a book he'd cut the pages out of to fit them inside. It was all so sweet until I opened the case and realized they were his choice. He didn't listen to me; he did what he wanted.

crushed

Bradley very much listened to me: he explained he'd found an Argentinian spot that had rave reviews for their soups. We stepped inside, and it was...quiet. It was a Wednesday night and very much not an LA hot spot. Instead, it was a little family restaurant with just a few seated throughout. Bradley gave our name, and the server smiled, directing us past empty tables to one with a reserved sign on it.

"You made a reservation?"

"Of course I did. There's good soup here too."

I looked down at the menu and saw Dr. Pepper, asking if he picked the place because it also served Dr. Pepper? It should be noted I used to *love* Dr. Pepper—like, would plan my McDonald's drive-thru location based on if it had Mr. Pibb or not (and if you're wondering, the one on Sunset and Laurel did not).

Bradley smiled at my mention of Dr. Pepper, and my heart did a little flip-flop at his complete thoughtfulness. The family restaurant was not okay with me only ordering soup and lovingly brought us out some of their favorite dishes on the house, so I did my best to take a bite of each one, even though at this point my stomach was basically Stonehenge. After dinner we drove up to Griffith Park, but it was already closed, so we just kept driving, talking the entire way. At one point I realized we were on my favorite stretch of LA. It's going from Pasadena to Burbank on the 134; if you go to the far-left lane and look out, it's full of lights twinkling in the hills and all over downtown. I would drive it every night my first year in LA, coming home from my retail store, still not believing I lived in LA. I looked over at Bradley, and as he

kiersten lyons

listened, I was starting to not be able to believe someone like him existed.

We just kept talking. All the way through the city, all the way to my place, all the way to my front door. We lingered, both not ready for the night to end. Bradley spoke first.

"I had a really good time."

"Me too."

"I really want to kiss you, but I've never kissed anyone on a first date."

His face registered such...what was it? It was definitely cute but not at all James's boyish charm; it was something else...something wholesome. Before I could figure it all out, I was back in my apartment, texting Amy about the whole night. But I didn't get a chance to finish it because up popped a text for me.

Tonight was amazing.

Bradley didn't do the standard three days wait—he didn't even wait until he got home. *Who was this guy?!*

⋆✳⋆

"I have something to tell you."

Bradley's voice was unsteady, nervous, so I became nervous. It was only the next night; what happened between then and now?

He held out a paper plate of chocolate covered strawberries. "I didn't want to do this over the phone, and they had some extra of these at work, so I thought I would... um..."

180

crushed

Is he about to tell me he has a secret family?

"Okay…?"

"Please take a strawberry. It'll make me feel less terrible."

Yeah, he has a secret family.

"I don't want a strawberry."

He shifted his weight and took a big breath in. "Okay, so you know last night, when you saw on the menu that they had Dr. Pepper? And you looked up from your menu and asked me if I specifically picked the restaurant because they had Dr. Pepper?"

I nodded.

"Well, I kind of shrugged and smiled, and I guess it implied that I did. I honestly didn't think much of it until you told me you called Amy and told her all about our first date and specifically how thoughtful it was that I chose a restaurant that had soup and Dr. Pepper, and I couldn't let whatever this is start off as a lie. I should have said no."

I stared at him. "You're saying you came here, in person, because you felt terrible that you *kind of* implied that you chose a restaurant because it had Dr. Pepper, and that actually wasn't true?"

He nodded, so ashamed.

And then I busted out laughing. To which he horrified.

"Bradley, that's the sweetest thing I've ever heard. Who are you? Like, are you even real?"

He was real, and honestly, I was having a bit of a hard time with it. Twenty minutes after he came over, we were sitting at a bar near each of our places grabbing a beer, and I

kiersten lyons

was studying his all-too-wholesome face. My stomach wasn't stone anymore; it wasn't even flip-floppy—it was just settled, and I wasn't sure how I felt about it.

I sipped my beer, knowing we'd spent the last month talking about anything and everything, we could talk about this:

"It's just… You call when you say you will. Same when you make plans. You keep them. I'm used to the chase—you know, the push and the pull…the butterflies. I'm scared you're just too nice."

Bradley nodded, taking it all in. Taking me in.

"So, it looks like I have two options: I can either treat you the way you're used to being treated—like crap—and then you'll like me more…or I can treat you, what? 'Nice,' but then you won't like me?"

I nodded, embarrassed to hear it repeated back to me. He nodded too, his almost three years of therapy and a lifetime of goodness showing through.

"Okay, so here's what I'm going to do: I'm going to keep being me, treating you the way you deserve to be treated, the way everyone deserves to be treated, and if you can't handle that, that's okay. I understand."

Uh… you heard that right? Of course you did because it was the most incredible thing a boy has ever said to any girl. Ever.

IN THE HISTORY OF THE WORLD.

A little while later we were back at my front door, back to not wanting the night to end. But this time felt different, it wasn't our first date, and even though that had been only twenty-four hours before, it felt like a lifetime had happened

crushed

in between. I was pretty sure my heart was going to leap out of my chest as he looked at me with such deep tenderness.

How had that face gotten even more wholesome?!

He leaned in to kiss my cheek, his fingers lightly touching mine, and with all the gumption a girl who's still getting over heartbreak could muster, I leaned in just a bit further, and our lips briefly touched. It was so sweet, but quick, until he pulled me back in—a month of bantering, of late-night conversations, of deep honesty wrapped me up in the hottest kiss I'd ever known. I completely forgot where I was.

But then, all of a sudden, I knew exactly, and I began giggling at the sheer confusion of how someone so kind and wholesome could be so good at this. The minute I giggled, Bradley pulled back in embarrassment, fearing the worst. But I pulled him close, whispering:

"Where the fuck did that come from?"

He laughed then too (with relief), scooping me up again, both of us laughing and kissing, and it was without a doubt way hotter than the back and forth of hoping the boy would just text back.

Chapter Eighteen

raising the green flag

"**I** just wish we could have one day where we don't talk about James."

"I know. I'm sorry. It's all so unfair."

I hated that this was our reality. Bradley's face registered hurt, yes, because so much still reminded me of James, but also hurt for me that this was my everyday whether I wanted it or not. I really did try so hard to get James out of my head.

I mean, yes of course I occasionally Facebook stalked him like any normal human being…

But for the most part I would have given anything to never think about him again. Yet no matter how hard I tried, so much in my day-to-day still could trigger a stinging memory. Especially as the anniversary of our engagement was fast approaching.

The anniversary of the forty-eight things…

Bradley had been helping me with an audition when something had triggered a reminder of James, which triggered Bradley's honesty. I asked him if he wanted me to not bring these moments up, but he shook his head. He was

crushed

grateful I felt safe enough to work through it, he also felt safe enough to tell me how hard it could be for him. It was a cycle we'd break eventually, but for now, it was still there, and we were still new.

I tried to switch us back to the audition sides (that's the scene an actor reads for the audition). It was for a casting director I hadn't seen in years, and I was nervous to say the least.

Casting directors in LA run the spectrum from super kind and welcoming to actors (think my friend Sara who got me my manager way back when) to those who are failed actors, relishing in their power over others. I have had great experiences and truly horrific ones. My audition with this guy years before was the latter.

From the moment I got in the room it was terrible. I was so new that I was immediately thrown off when the CD didn't even look up or acknowledge I was there, just looked over my barren resume, muttering to himself, "Why did I even bring you in?"

He then asked me if I was ready, I nodded yes (feeling anything but), and then he proceeded to bark orders at me before I'd even uttered one word. My last line in the scene was supposed to be me yelling "No!" and in such a state of out of body, I raised my fist, shaking it, as I cried out "NOoooooooo!" somehow with it sounding almost British.

IT. WAS. MORTIFYING.

It was also years before, such a small moment, and yet I still felt so small. Bradley watched me act it all out as I laughed, equally embarrassed and delighted at the end bit.

kiersten lyons

Being an actor really is just a dance between the two. So is being a human.

I woke up the morning of the audition to a text from Bradley to make sure I checked my windshield before I headed to the audition.

Yeah, like I'm gonna wait until then to check it...

I bounded down my apartment building's stairs to find an index card addressed to the casting director. I laughed at the thought of me handing the note to this power-hungry casting director and saying, "My boyfriend wanted you to have this."

Did I just call him my boyfriend?

I stopped laughing as I read Bradley's words. He instructed the casting director to look up, then noted many of my recent guest stars, telling the CD how talented I was and what a fool he'd be if he didn't give me the role.

I walked into that audition with the note safely tucked inside my pocket, and Bradley fully tucked in my heart.

"No way *that* guy, with *those* hands, is a virgin."

Chris, Kristen, and I were at Rand's forty-second annual Christmas party (although to be fair it was only the third one—but adding decades just made it feel more festive). Also, to be fair: Bradley has huge hands.

Bradley had come to pick me up, and Chris was already excited to meet him; he had heard a few stories from me (item one: "Kiersten, how's he feel with your whole no-sex-until-marriage thing?").

crushed

Chris would always say, "Kiersten, the minute you moved to LA, you dropped your bags and yelled out: 'I'm not having sex until marriage!'"

Well, you know, except for that whole Brian year and the "I'm angry and don't care what happens to me" grief time, but also, Chris wasn't wrong. After so many years of getting rejected over it, I thought if I put it out there right at the beginning, I could stop the rejection.

I also apparently told everyone I wasn't pretty enough. It's as if I had a bunch of labels stamped all over on my forehead, and I was so sure each of them walked in the room way before me. Especially *loser*—that one was always the one I was dying to get rid of. Dying to prove wrong.

Bradley had asked me if I wanted him to come to the party with me, but I was scared. It was scary to be vulnerable, scary to introduce someone new to old friends. Chris was protective of me, and he had given James a bit of an easy time since they had mutual friends and look how great that turned out. But I needn't have been worried, because from the minute they met, Chris liked him, because he liked the way Bradley liked me. Plus, it didn't hurt that minutes before Bradley turned up, I had told Chris, Kristen, and Rand all about the box.

Just a few days before Rand's party, Bradley had come over holding a box. It was finally December 14, 2009. One year to the day that James proposed. Three hundred and sixty-five days since the forty-eight tiny details.

"I know you're not looking forward to today, and I wanted to make sure you had these."

kiersten lyons

As sweet and funny as Bradley was, and as much self-reflection, self-love, and self-work I had done, I was still sad. December 14 just held pain. There was no other way around it. Plus, days before, James had won that reality show, and so no matter how much I tried to remind myself he didn't get to hold those forty-eight details, everything in me screamed how much of a winner he always was and how much of a loser I'd always be.

"Just open it."

It was a candle box, that smelled like…wait, was that tobacco? I scrunched up my nose without thinking, and Bradley laughed, explaining it was the only box he could find. He was moonlighting as a reviewer for his friend's lifestyle blog and would often get random stuff sent to him.

I opened the box slowly.

"I cut most from magazines and mailers," he said.

I reached in, finding dozens of words, many in his handwriting. Words like "brave" and "beautiful," "funny" and "unique" stared back.

crushed

"These are truths," he continued. "About you. No matter what happens with us, you deserve to know the truth."

I stared at the tiny pieces of paper, not wanting to look up, not ready to cry in front of another boy, but having no choice because I saw it:

kiersten lyons

I won't pretend at that moment that I was all healed—it would take years for me to unravel the knots of putting my worth in others' hands—but in that moment, I began to believe I was worth it. You are too.

So worth it.

Chapter Nineteen

a real-life romcom

Bradley and I went to each of our respective childhood hometowns for Christmas.

We'd been dating less than two months, calm down...

I, on the other hand, could not calm down, because I was beyond excited for him to open his gift. We'd decided to wait until Christmas Day to open each other's presents over Skype.

Yeah, I said Skype.

He called my computer, but I couldn't get upstairs fast enough before my entire family heard the ringing and soon faces were popping into frame. Within what felt like thirty seconds it seemed our entire families were onscreen: my parents, his parents, siblings, and a partridge in a pear tree. None of them knew each other, and yet here they all were saying hi, all so excited to meet. Okay, to be fair, Bradley and my sisters had already met, as the twins were going to college in LA. Upon their initial meeting Bradley noted:

kiersten lyons

"I feel like I have no questions about anything now that I've been locked in a car with you and your sisters as you drive around LA belting out the *Newsies* soundtrack."

But this was different; this was parents and Christmas and him opening my small present in front of literally EVERYONE. Suddenly, my delight in being onstage vanished, and I felt beyond exposed. I wanted to hide, to crawl away, to run—but I had no choice but to sit there as Bradley opened the gift I was so sure would just be between us.

But what in my life am I ever sure of that actually happens?!

He unwrapped the paper, his eyes studying the wooden box I had found with a quote from his favorite movie, *Willy Wonka & the Chocolate Factory*. His mom was beside herself as he opened the lid and inside was a card stating that I couldn't believe he's the guy from that improv class years before and still couldn't believe someone like him existed. I was so hoping he wouldn't read it, and he didn't, but in true romcom fashion his family read it over his shoulder.

"Oh, that's so sweet."

Tucked underneath the note was a little memento I had swiped from his desk. See that very night, on Christmas, Bradley's first ever guest star on CBS's "Till Death" was airing. I was so proud—that first time your face is on TV is such a big deal for most actors and I got the box in the hopes it could be a place to store all his future mementos and treasures that would soon pile up as he made his way through the business…

He just kept turning the box over and over asking how I found a box with his favorite quote, I was beyond excited he

crushed

liked it as he urged me to open mine, prefacing it was not as thoughtful as mine.

"You already gave me the most thoughtful gift!"

His mom was too eager to hear what that was, but I was already holding up his gift: a long pendant necklace with a... red stone.

"Because red's your favorite color."

Oh right, I forgot to tell him I didn't love the color red...or that daisy....

I knew over Skype with our families wasn't the time, but I also knew I needed to tell him. Not only because if we worked out, I might end up with so many red things, but more so because I didn't want another relationship where I made it all about the other person and their needs.

The night we both got back in town, he invited me over for dinner. He was cooking, and I was a hot mess trying to figure out how to tell him I loved the thoughtfulness of the flower and the necklace, but I didn't love the red.

Ever so gently I began to tell him how grateful I was, how the note on my car and the box of truths that I was starting to refer to as the "Bradley Box" were both incredible. Perfection really. But I had to be honest in that I didn't really like red, and I'm not a big fan of gerbera daisies.

He laughed. "I swear you said that was your favorite color."

I shook my head, relieved he wasn't mad.

"Why would I be mad?"

I didn't want to bring up James again, but it felt like it made too much sense not to. So, I gently explained how anytime I brought anything like this up to James, he would immediately get angry, sometimes even cruel. Bradley looked at me, nodding along, listening so intently.

That damn wholesome face....

He then popped up from the couch, looking for his phone and asking if he could play me a song. He explained he had heard it on the flight home, and all of a sudden he'd realized how I could still be so hurt by James yet really wanting to be all in with him. I nodded as he pressed play, and the first notes of A Fine Frenzy's "Near to You" played. Each line was better than the last; it was as if she had taken detailed notes on the last year of my life.

I felt so seen.

I began to cry, and not the sweet tears like I had cried from the Bradley Box. These were deep ones that came from months of pain, and from the relief of being so seen. I apologized, but Bradley just wrapped his arms around me and didn't let me go, as I let go.

The song ended, but I stayed there wrapped up in Bradley a little longer, for the first time in a long time, feeling so safe.

I knew I was in love with Bradley weeks before I told him.

It was just after that night with the color red honesty and the song and me crying snotty tears into his shoulder. Throughout the whole time we'd been dating, I hadn't spoken to Ashley. I had tried. Tried calling, texting, even reaching out to Ashley's family, but nothing. I was trying to keep calm;

crushed

she was a teenager now, and Littles often don't want to spend as much time with their Bigs at that age, but when our new caseworker called to say he too hadn't been able to connect with her, I got worried.

Since meeting five and half years before, we'd never gone this long without contact, and I was starting to feel sick. Ashley lived in South LA. Her life and mine were so different, and concern for her safety was a pretty normal response. Bradley saw how worried I was getting and asked me if he could pray for us, and as much as I wanted anyone and everyone to pray for Ashley, I was also like, "Uhh, praying's my thing dude; I'm the one who brings up God in relationships."

Him praying made me feel vulnerable and...not in control. I didn't like that. But I also loved Ashley, so I gratefully nodded. He prayed, and it wasn't too long, but enough that I knew he truly meant every word. A few days later I got a call from our case worker. Ashley was safe, she was okay, and her Granny wanted me to call her. The whole time I was on the phone with the case worker, Bradley's face registered as what I can only describe as invested—his eyebrows popping up, looking for hope, as I nodded it was okay.

"I know we were going to grab lunch, but I need to call her Granny and—"

"Absolutely."

I called Granny right away and heard her slow, soothing voice letting me know Ashley was fine. The relief of knowing she was safe was one I would know many times over the next decade and one in that moment brought tears to my eyes, which only bubbled up more when I looked over to Bradley.

kiersten lyons

He, at that moment, was outside on my little deck, sweeping the leaves. I was writing a new script, all about camp, and he knew how much I wanted to have a little outside corner devoted to writing. I hadn't had the time yet to set it up, but here he was, fully cleaning it and giving me space to talk to Granny.

Aaaand I love him.

I was now full-on crying as I got off the phone with Granny. Bradley looked up, seeing the tears and fearing the worst. I laughed at his concerned face.

"I'm fine, really, and so is Ashley. But you...you cleaned my little deck."

"Yeah, I wanted you to have a place to write. That's so important to you."

Chapter Twenty

bye bye bye

"**Y**eah, what was up with you calling and asking me to sleep with you? You were joking, right?"

I was sitting across from James inside a little lunch spot off Melrose, ten months after he told me he didn't love me, seven months since I made that call, and five months since Bradley and I had started dating.

"Yeah, I definitely wasn't joking."

His eyes widened as I told him how serious I had been.

How that September I had been squarely in my "self-destructive" phase, as days before I made that call, I had been in Nashville hanging out with a singer-songwriter I had met on his way through Maine. In my anger, I slept with him, and *spoiler alert*: it did everything in the short run to help me feel not like a loser and everything in the long run to pile onto the pain. He was funny and cute and talented, so I was *sure* he would see how great I was and stop hooking up with random girls in random cities.

Pro-Tip: Crying over two guys simultaneously is gut wrenching—I don't recommend.

kiersten lyons

Then I came back to LA, and Brian happened to visit town, and I just so happened to sleep with him. After not having sex for four years, I had gotten back on the wagon, if you will, trying to get back at James, trying to get back at God, trying to get back my worth.

"You had sex with Brian again?"

I nodded. I could tell it was killing James—it was the thing that had always killed him—that I had slept with Brian and wouldn't with him. It admittedly felt altogether delicious to see him squirm like this.

But that's not why I was at this lunch; it wouldn't offer any sort of peace to sit in this revenge. I took a breath, trying to get back the plot.

"So, no, I was very much not joking. Plus, I was sure if you and I finally had sex, then you would think I was enough."

Months of Al-Anon, tons of work, and beginning to love myself for who I am had given me this moment, and I wasn't going to throw it away on making myself feel good and making him feel like shit.

He looked at me with all his boyish charm. "Oh, yeah. We never had sex."

Except now that I was months sober from him, it wasn't charming—it was just performative. I knew he remembered it, and I knew it killed him that we hadn't. It was *the* topic of conversation our entire relationship, yet he was acting as if it had just slipped his mind.

crushed

I told him I was seeing someone new, and he said he was too. "But I mean, we're both so busy we hardly see each other, so it's not really anything much."

I stared at him. His tone was like that of a bad child actor. Even though he was a good six inches taller than me, he looked small sitting across the table, unable to tell the truth. Unable to tell me it was serious (they would go on to get engaged before the end of the year).

He just looked little.

By the time James and I were at lunch, I'd been trying to sell my wedding dress for months. At first, I couldn't possibly. The sting of even knowing it was hanging in a closet at my parents' back home was too much. But little by little, I was becoming more ready to let go, more ready to close the door on this whole time. I had been calling wedding resell shops, but each one offered less than the previous. It wasn't like it was an especially expensive dress (well, to me, french fry–sharing girl, it was, but in the grand scheme of the wedding world and a trust fund groom, it was next to nothing). Which worked out quite perfectly because when the first deposit was needed, I was still waiting on a paycheck, and James offered to cover it. And when the final amount was due, he'd already called off the wedding, already broken my heart over for two weeks straight. So, when the shop asked if I wanted to put the remainder on the credit card on file I was all, "Yup!"

kiersten lyons

I looked at him across the table, pushing around his mixed greens salad, and asked if he wanted whatever the resale shop offered me for the dress. It seemed odd for me to keep his money, even if would be just a couple hundred dollars. He shook his head.

"No, it's yours."

"Can you take off your sunglasses? I want to look you in the eyes when I say this."

James and I were now standing just outside the lunch spot, beside my car, swapping things we had of each other's. I pulled up the small crate that had been sitting in my closet, piled high with his old journals, so grateful to finally be free of the weight of carrying his past. His old life he had given me, and I had finally realized it was never mine to hold, never mine to carry.

When we were breaking up, his best friend told me, "I think you and James were more like mother-son than actual partners—he was always looking for you to fill something."

I'd gotten defensive, but standing there in the grass, handing over James' past, I saw it now. At first, James was almost high off the love I gave him, it filled something up in him, but after a while it couldn't, no matter how much I loved him, no matter how many times I offered him grace. Because we can't fix someone else, no matter how many movies tell us we can. We're not God. We're not a higher power. We're all just human.

crushed

James handed me a Brita water filter, the only thing he had of mine. Which is hilarious and ridiculous that he thought I had been waiting ten months to get it back. From the moment he broke my heart, I dreamed about the day he would finally make amends, finally realize what he did and truly be sorry, truly change. Now, holding out this water filter, and thinking back to the wedding dress, I realized this was it. This was the most he could give me.

"You hurt me so deeply, and I won't ever be the same, but I forgive you because I don't want to hold anger for you anymore. I literally *need* to forgive you."

It wasn't because some cult told me to, or even a twelve-step program. It wasn't because of church or the Bible or just "being the good girl" I always was.

It was because of that afternoon in Phoenix, ten months before, when the woman held me and told me I was loved. When she stayed there beside me so I wouldn't be alone. When she softly told me to tell God my pain. Because the more I told the truth, the more I saw the truth.

Closure wasn't given by the one who hurt me, but by the One who loves me.

As much as James had asked me to hold—his past, his wounds, his pain—I was now asking him to hold mine. My anger, my pain, my hatred for him. And it wasn't his to hold, because he couldn't. The way he was still pretending, the way he was still performing, he could never make amends the way I deeply hoped he would. I had to stop hoping in that, in him, and only then could I be released of the anguish.

kiersten lyons

It didn't mean he didn't hold responsibility for the hurt he caused, the cruelness he made me endure; it meant that was between him and God now. I didn't want it. It didn't serve me. In fact, it was crippling me.

So, I gave it to the One who could hold it, the One who was offering me grace. And I needed all the grace, because I never should have gotten back together with James in the first place. Please hear me: I'm not saying it's my fault that James hurt me, that he cheated, and that he was cruel. I mean because of how deeply I hurt, I allowed myself to be hurt so deeply, over and over.

When we were breaking up, I told Amy, I was so sure the whole relationship had been for James. It allowed him to see how truly loved he was. Amy looked at me with such care, "Kiersten, what if this about how much you needed to know the same?"

I had gotten defensive with her too, because of course I already knew, but as I stood there, I realized how right she had been.

It was time to stop the cycle of trying to prove my worth by getting others to see it.

Chapter Twenty-One

the sweetest redemption

Right before the Thanksgiving holiday later that year, I booked a guest star on a Fox show called *Bones*. Just in case you don't read my bio in this book, yes, I was wanted for the murder of my husband I shared with my sister wives.

You know, supes casual…

So here I was in full sister-wife attire: long dress, large bow, large family, sauntering over to visit a friend who worked on the Fox lot. The minute I got there, I jokingly held out my hand for her to see the massive ring the props department had given me, to which she said, "Oh, thank God, I had no idea how I was going to tell you…"

"Tell me what?"

"James is engaged, but it's okay now, because you are too."

"I'm not, this is just a props ring. I mean, I'm wearing a full-length sister wife dress."

kiersten lyons

She felt terrible, I felt worse…or did I? I told her it was fine and immediately called Bradley. It wasn't as if we hadn't talked about it; we had—very intentionally actually. I had left that summer to nanny in England with the family, and by the time I got back, he was all, "Well that was terrible, and I never want to be away from you that long again…" and I was all, "Don't you dare say things like that unless you actually mean it."

I might have been a bit scared at the moment…

Bradley picked up the phone as I calmly let him know that I just heard James got engaged the weekend before and I was trying to figure out how I felt about it. Not that he was engaged, but just that the person who cheated on me and almost destroyed my heart was allowed to be happy.

Forgiveness is sometimes a daily adventure…

Bradley was so patient as my thoughts swirled, but then they stopped because in reality I didn't care. I actually was hopeful for James, hopeful that maybe he did tell the truth at least once: when he said I taught him what actual unconditional love was. Hopeful that he could go and have a happy life. Hopeful that I was already in the middle of mine.

I had no idea how "in the middle of mine" I really was. You see, Bradley had originally planned to propose the next day, but because of *Bones*'s shooting schedule, he had to quickly pivot it all to the day after the holiday. We were spending Thanksgiving in Monterey with Parker and some friends, and he literally ran into the house before me to whisper-yell, "We're not engaged yet!" because he realized some of our friends might not have seen his covert texts.

crushed

The morning after Thanksgiving, we headed out to San Francisco to meet up with some PR people. Bradley was creating more and more content for his friend's lifestyle blog and had a car he was reviewing for this trip. He had new cars often to review, even Audi's here and there. This time he wanted to head towards the Golden Gate Bridge for a shot his editor wanted in the video.

I had asked him the day before for details about what we were doing in SF, but he kept being so casual about everything—which was *very* unlike Bradley. I was starting to think something was up and just looked at him, me smirking, him staring right back, not revealing anything. So that morning he told me he prayed God would make me stupid for the day, which I think is the funniest prayer ever because I'm a literal genius.

But the prayer worked, as he began to have more details, and I began to think I was wrong. We drove across the bridge, finding a spot on the Marin side to shoot. I helped him set up the shot and then pressed record as he started talking into camera all about the car. He did a few takes and then goes, "Hey, my editor was wondering if you'd get in the shot—he's heard some of the notes you've given me, and he thought it would be good to get you on camera."

I thought that sounded weird, but God made me stupid that day because your girl suspected NOTHING. Bradley started talking about the car and then turned to me and started talking about me.

Uh...what?

"I'm taken with you."

kiersten lyons

The corners of his eyes were crinkling up, and I realized he was getting emotional. I mean, Bradley loves cars, but not this much. I realized what was happening as everything he said got fuzzy, and everything around us got blurry. I watched his face—it was still so wholesome, but also so, so confident. He pulled out the ring, and at that moment I remembered I never gave him a size, so he'd snuck in an old one to the jewelers, but it was actually really old and so the engagement ring was tight, but I didn't care—it was perfect.

The whole thing was: the scrapbook he had made with receipts from our first dates, notes I had sent him, and even the notecards with the speech he had just made that he had forgotten most of and that I hadn't really heard a word of. Like I said, perfect. Not so perfect was the car being broken into later that day.

So apparently, like fifth grade, I am still easy to steal from....

We were heartbroken because not only did they get Bradley's laptop and backpack but also the camera he'd just recorded our proposal on. We headed in super late to our dinner reservations, the saddest newly engaged couple you've ever seen. It was comical. That night we fell asleep listening to the audio recording of the proposal (the robbers hadn't found the mic pack) holding hands, the ring safely on.

The next morning as the glass repair guys finished up, we found the camera on the seat, buried under the broken glass, just waiting to be seen.

crushed

✶

Bradley and I got married Memorial Day weekend, two years from those two horrible weeks in May. Exactly two years from that Saturday tearfully rushed away from the feather-plumed wedding right into an engagement session. Wait, take that back—two engagement sessions.

I had found the most beautiful wedding dress, but it was more than four times my budget, and that made it completely out of the question. I would study it often, trying to find a dupe of some sort, and then one day it clicked—it was the same silhouette as the one that was still hanging in my parents' closet, still waiting to be sold. I looked up my dress online and realized I still loved it, not because it had anything to do with James but because it had everything to do with me.

I asked Bradley what he thought about me wearing the dress, knowing how much James infiltrated that first part of our relationship. I explained how every time I saw the dress, even thought about it, it was me in it walking to him. I did want to add to it just a bit, the same details that the expensive dress had. He asked for a little time to think about it and came back a couple of days later.

"I love the idea of you wearing the dress. It feels like so much of our relationship, God redeeming such pain to such beauty. I also love that you want to add to it a little."

Then he just looked at me with such wholesomeness that I blurted out, "No but seriously, WHO ARE YOU?!"

He laughed. "Plus, James paid for it. What a guy!"

kiersten lyons

Now standing in the dress in the bridal suite, I couldn't believe how right Bradley was. It wasn't just the dress, or the day being redeemed; it was a lifetime of believing I knew exactly what I needed, when really, I was surprised over and over with the best of life's gifts.

And it wasn't just the dates or the dress; Emmy's daughter, the one I chased bunnies with that horrible day, was our flower girl. Parker was doing one reading, my big brother, Luke, the other, and good ol' Chris was singing our first dance.

Right before I walked down the aisle, I was given a gift from Bradley. I've seen groom's gift diamond earrings or a necklace, but Bradley gave me something even more priceless: laughter.

Because he gave me one red gerbera daisy.

If someone had told me, "Two years from these two weeks right now, while you're in terrible pain, is going to be one of the greatest moments of your life," I would've punched them in the throat. Because that is a cruel and horrible joke, and how dare you?

But it was the truth. And it gets even better.

Two years after that, literally four years to the *day* I was told I was unlovable, on the exact third Sunday in May, our daughter was born. God redeemed that day; it no longer holds pain because I get to hold her.

crushed

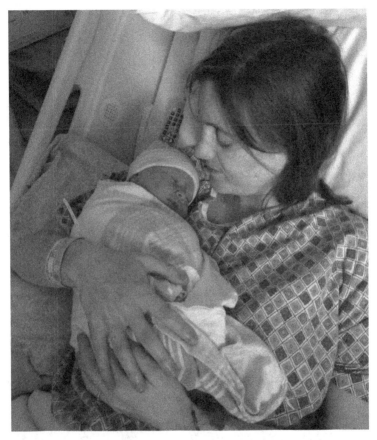

And I truly believe I had hope because that woman, so many years ago in a church, held me.

It may look as if my life just got tied up in a sweet little bow, but the truth is, that ribbon still had a lot of knots in it. And let's not get it twisted; this is not what I wanted. Bradley was never on my MASH. The guy I couldn't have always was.

Any of them, all of them, most especially James. How else could I prove my worth? It killed me to lose him, it killed me to forgive him, it killed me to kill my idea of a perfect life.

But it was just that—an idea. The reality was just a little boy who stood there, holding a Brita filter, squinting in the sun, looking hugely relieved I had just forgiven him. Almost like he could finally brush off what happened. It was over now.

James, the guy who couldn't tell the truth, gave me possibly the greatest gift of truth: that what we *want* isn't always what is *good*. And what is good can be so hard to want at first, but always, always worth it.

Because goodness always stands there, with eyes wide open.

Chapter Twenty-Two

big sister

I'm not saying if you become a Big Sister, you'll one day meet Taylor Swift and make her cry, but I'm also not saying you won't....

In the year of our Lord 2011, I was back in the Beverly Center working, not in retail, but grabbing some strapless bra options for my boss (which sounds weird, but when you're a personal assistant, nothing is weird). I had met my now boss when I was guest starring on that episode of *Bones* as a sister wife. But as well as my career was going, I was still not able to pay my bills with it, thus buying bras for others was needed.

I was leaving Victoria's Secret when I noticed her, cascading blonde curls, holding her own shopping bag, looking about. I walked past her, knowing the kindest thing I could do was give her privacy, but then pivoted, realizing I had so much to thank her for.

"Hi—I just quickly wanted to say thank you."

Taylor looked up, a bit confused, "Thank you?"

kiersten lyons

"Yeah, I'm just really grateful for your music. I mean, your song 'White Horse' was integral in helping grieve when my ex called off our wedding."

Right after camp, right before going to Nashville, I visited my best friend from camp at UGA. She'd showed me around, introduced me to sweet tea, and practically shoved a mix CD in my hands before I drove off to Nashville.

"Number seven. White Horse. Trust me."

She was twenty, so obviously her music tastes had to be trusted. And she wasn't wrong. Even now the opening chords put me right back to driving in the south, right back to that summer.

Taylor was looking at me with such genuine compassion. "I'm so sorry."

"Thank you, but really, it's more about your song 'Fifteen.'"

"'Fifteen?'"

"I'm a Big Sister through Big Brothers Big Sisters, and my Little Sister and I love it. It's sparked so many conversations. We sing it at the top of our lungs, and we belt it out in traffic. So, thank you for creating a song that two girls from such different backgrounds and generations can both be so affected by."

"Wait, are you serious?"

crushed

"Yeah, we listen to it every Friday. Fridays are our days to hang out—grab ice cream, see a movie, that kind of thing. Anyway, I just wanted to say hi. I don't want to take up anymore of your time."

"No, wait—thank you for coming up and telling me that, and thank you for being a Big Sister." Her voice catching, she said, "Can I give you a hug?"

We hugged, and as I pulled back, we both had tears in our eyes. "I'm Kiersten, by the way."

"I'm Taylor."

I smiled, touched by her humility. "I know."

I texted Ashley as soon as I got out of the store. She asked if I got a picture, and I laughed, realizing I hadn't even thought of it.

"Kiki, how could you not think of it!"

I told her maybe one day we will, when she's there too.

Weeks before Ashley's eighteenth birthday, she was set to move in with Bradley, my daughter, and me. It was months from her high school graduation, and we thought it'd be a great chance for a fresh start, and I was sure our landlord would feel the same.

"So, Ashley'd move into the spare bedroom, and we're so excited to be able to—"

"I'm going to stop you right there. She can't move in with you. You can't have three people in the house."

kiersten lyons

"But there already are three people in the house: Bradley and I, our infant. Plus, last summer my little sisters lived with us after graduation, and I—"

"I'm not allowing another person on the lease."

"Oh no, we're not charging her rent. We're paying for everything. You can even *up* our rent—she just needs a safe and stable place to—"

"No. She can't move in. I've worked in real estate long enough, and this isn't a good business decision. I know it sounds cruel, but that's my answer and we're not talking about it anymore."

In less than three minutes, every single plan our little family had made came crashing down—and in such an abrupt way. It was nothing short of heartbreaking. And familiar.

Here's the thing about the familiar, the triggers, and the "I've been here before."

THEY SUCK.

All at once you're right back to finding it hard to breathe, crying at the unfairness, questioning how another thing could change so terribly fast, because the person is being so terribly cruel. And it doesn't matter if your therapist reminds you the only thing constant in life is change, because that shit is just rude.

But it's true, because here's the other thing about the familiar, the triggers, and the "I've been here before."

YOU KNOW WHAT TO DO.

I don't mean how to fix it; I mean how to live it. Because this isn't your first rodeo, you can look back and let the other ones remind you that you're going to be okay. Because if we let them, the triggers have the ability to be the balm.

crushed

It doesn't mean you don't cry out at the unfairness of it all, the swift end. We did. I cried something fierce. We loved that little house (and not just because of the cheap rent). It was in the cutest neighborhood (we could walk to Trader Joe's!) that had the dreamiest backyard with ivy climbing the detached garage (and no, one-third of it was not an apartment). The house had an orange tree with a dictator of a squirrel that almost never let us pick an orange. We even let ourselves dare to dream of maybe buying it one day, and now that wasn't even an option.

I mean, I guess it could have been, if I called Ashley up and said, "Hey, never mind what we talked about, you can't move in anymore. We love this grouping of bricks too much." And to be fair, we did love those bricks; we just loved her more. SO MUCH MORE.

So heartbroken and unsteady, still feeling as if the wind was knocked out of us, we set out to find any place with three bedrooms—house, townhouse, apartment. It was as if I was circling things on my MASH sheet once again, just desperate to find something safe we could afford. We only had weeks, as Ashley was moving in when she turned eighteen, but the more we looked, the more it became desperate, and I became angrier.

How could our landlord not care? How do people treat others so casually, so cruelly?

At the last minute, we found one with three bedrooms in a safe neighborhood, but it was seven hundred dollars more a month (not to mention a large deposit). Where would we get seven hundred dollars more a month?! Struggling for breath

kiersten lyons

and any sense of hope, I did the only I knew to do. The only thing that would bring offer peace. I went back to that church in my head (not physically—I was in LA, and that was Phoenix). I closed my eyes and put my hand to my chest, desperate to slow my racing heart, desperate to hear the kind woman's words once again.

Keep telling Him your pain.

It wasn't as if I hadn't been since I'd hung up with the landlord; it was that this time it was coupled with the knowledge only those who have had their world blown up know. To finally find peace, to rest in hope, the only option is letting go of everything we thought *should* happen to allow what is in front of us. We know goodness will come, even when we don't want it. And so, I prayed, "Look, we've got nothing left. If You want us to bring Ashley in, you've got to figure this out."

We got an email a bit later. Our new SAG health insurance had come through (Bradley had a commercial running and we barely squeaked in on the minimum qualifying amount), and we'd just received the new monthly bill, and it was less. How much you ask?

Seven hundred dollars less.

Sure, it was a miracle, but also annoying because it was not what I wanted. Not what I hoped for.

Or You could have just changed our stupid landlord's heart!

But apparently that is up to her (because of free will, blah, blah, blah), and so we humbly signed the lease, grateful for a safe and miraculously affordable home for our little family. Before we even had moved in, when we were on our

crushed

first walk through, both Bradley and I felt like the front bedroom was Ashley's. It had big windows and lots of light—and I'm not exactly sure why, because she hadn't specifically mentioned anything, but we just randomly felt it was right. A few Fridays later, I picked her up to see the new house, just me and her, just like it had been for the last eight and half years.

Big Sister. Little Sister.

"Kiki, this one is mine? My own room? With windows? I have windows?"

Giving up what we want is hard, but it is always worth it. Always.

I won't pretend I didn't grieve our life in that little house just two miles away, long for the neighbors, that backyard, or those walks to Trader Joe's, but I would give it all up again and again to see her face when she saw those windows.

And just like everything my therapist said, change again came. Rudely and abruptly. Over and over.

A few months later, with no work in sight, B took a job in Arizona, and I stayed in LA with our girls. Ashley needed to finish high school in the amazing charter school we'd just gotten her into (with the help of a dear friend), and at that point, I still thought I was selling a TV show to a major network. Besides, it was only three months before we'd all join him in Phoenix.

Except right at the last minute, Los Angeles Unified School District changed their graduation requirements, and Ashley would need to be there for the full school year to grad-

kiersten lyons

uate. Nine months. And that producer who wanted to help me sell the TV show? Well, you already know he eventually ghosted me.

And for the record, I don't recommend, while your dreams are dying and life is fully shifting so rapidly, doing it all with your partner a state away. I don't recommend having to watch someone you love so dearly think she has just three more months to complete a dream she had fought so hard for and then have to grapple with it being three times that. I don't recommend solo parenting an eighteen-month-old and an eighteen-year-old at the same time. I don't recommend paying two rents, in two states, in two time zones.

But I do recommend this:

crushed

⋆⚹⋆

"I'm going to go on break. My mom's here, and we're having lunch."

Ashley was at her new job at Chick-fil-A, and she had just called me *Mom*.

No, it's chill. I'm not getting completely emotional right now. And I'm definitely not blinking back tears. I'm just a girl just standing here, holding a chicken sandwich in a foil bag, like whatever, normal day…

I didn't set out to be her other mom—that was never part of the plan—but like everything in my life, in all our lives, the best things don't come in plans or goals but in people. We were just supposed to give her a place for a few months to help her graduate, a place to save up so she could set out on her own, and honestly, I was just excited about having someone to watch TV with.

"Hey Ashley, want to watch *Downton Abbey* again?"

She looked at me, eyebrows up. "The one with all the white people crying? Nah, I'm good."

We laughed for probably four minutes straight, and I've never looked at *Downton* the same, but I've also never looked at anything the same. Ashley would sometimes say living with us changed her, but it was also us who were changed. Our sweet girl marked our life, and we couldn't think of anything more honoring than forever marking that mark. Her ink told her story, and now it would tell ours, because Bradley and I would be getting our first tattoos, which read:

June 16th.

kiersten lyons

The day she walked, in full cap and gown, across that stage.

For years I carried a lot of anger towards that landlord, huge resentment towards her hard heart, her shutting us down, not even wanting to discuss the possibility. But now I just hold sadness for her, because she never got to know Ashley.

That landlord never sat in a room as our sweet girl hilariously told a story from work or watched her squirm when you shower her with compliments. She never got to see Ashley dance with her nieces and nephews or chat with her Granny that she holds so dear.

She never got to see the magic that is Ashley unfold.

Because isn't that the greatest gift of love? The constant unfolding of beauty? Who cares about business when you get the chance to show up in someone's life? Nothing about loving someone well is anything other than the *best* decision. I met Ashley almost twenty years ago; she started calling me her other mom nine years after that, and I am very aware that if James and I had stayed together, had gotten married, there is no way the latter would've happened.

And not just because he always chose the easy and the comfortable, but because I would've been working so hard to make us work, trying so hard to get him to see me, that I wouldn't have been able to truly see anyone else.

I very much realize the privilege that is Bradley, the gift of who he is and the way we loves me, but I also hope that we honor what we have by honoring others. Because I don't

crushed

ever want to choose the easy, the comfortable. I never want to choose a grouping of bricks over a human.

I pray I always choose love. Always.

Chapter Twenty-Three

that time i challenged taylor swift

My intent is not to anger Swifties with this title. I *am* one—hello, just last chapter I made her cry happy tears. Nor am I trying to get some pull quote that might give the book press: "Unknown former actress calls out global superstar!"

Not at all. I love Taylor. Truly. But real love isn't just agreeing with everything the other says, blindly following the status quo. Real, genuine, healthy love is a give and take. It allows us to ask questions, disagree, and challenge one another.

You know, the opposite of a cult.

And more than that, I think we deserve more than what we've been offered—what Taylor's been offered. I think we deserve the truth.

I was sitting on the floor of our apartment when the teaser came on *The Today Show*.

crushed

Up next: Taylor's acceptance speech for the 2021 BRITs Global Icon award.

I wasn't thinking much of it. Two months into moving, we were still getting settled.

Oh yeah, we had moved again (actually, *again* again), and the commercial break was ending and onscreen was Taylor. She was absolutely glowing, looking at the crowd with all the authority a Grammy Award–winning, platinum-selling, once-in-a-generation artist has. She powerfully spoke, encouraging the audience that in every career there will be naysayers. That no matter what path we choose, we will be with people who do not want us to succeed. That we can believe so deeply, care so much, and still people will say negate what we're doing.

"But you can't let that crush you. You have to let that fuel you. We live in a world where anyone can say anything that they want about you at any time. But just please remember that you have the right to prove them wrong."

The entire audience erupted in cheers, literally some yelling with their hands cupped on their mouths like they were screaming for Michael Phelps's final swim. And it was and is an Olympic-level last line. Truly an absolute mic drop.

It's also absolute bullshit.

And I know you might want to throw this book across the room at my saying this. I get it. Part of me wants to, too. Because part of me wants it to be true.

I always will. Because years before Taylor wrote "Mean"— heck, just mere months after Taylor was *born*, I was sitting on my bed looking into those *Tonight Show* cameras. Decades

kiersten lyons

before she made this speech, I dreamed of making the same one, standing on stage holding up an award and yelling out, "Prove them wrong!"

And I know I'm not the only one.

Because who hasn't recited the "Big mistake—*huge*," scene from *Pretty Woman* like a thousand times? Who hasn't dreamed of looking at the person who wronged us, who are now standing in shock at how wonderful we truly are as we yell out what a mistake they made? HUGE!

There's a reason that Susan Boyle's first audition has 268 million views on just one account alone. A reason we crave those moments when the cruel judge is left in awe, the mean girls are put in their place, the whole room is humbled. Because who doesn't want to prove to those who mocked us, who cast us off, who told us we didn't matter that they were wrong?

But if we ever truly want to have hope, truly have peace, we have to want more than the life Taylor's proposing. The life every single one of those artists were cheering about.

The life I lived.

And, yes, just in case no one's told you, it does feel incredible to, from *Jimmy Kimmel Live*'s green room, call the boy who mocked you, your acting dreams, your lack of puberty, your fashion choice of a thrifted scarf around your neck for a solid thirty minutes during sophomore year English, to let him know the sketch you filmed with a massive hip-hop star would be on network TV that night.

Okay, I didn't actually call Lyndsay, since I didn't have his number (and was also so scared), so instead I called one of his best friends because I knew it would get back to him.

crushed

Like whatever, nbd, I'm just the best at being chill...

As Jimmy introduced my sketch, the entire green room turned toward me. Within seconds they were laughing, and before the sketch was even over, I was being approached by people. Important people, people who made decisions and had nothing to do with elementary school or high school or that dance when Sam G. told me I looked like a flat-chested alien.

Because here, in this green room, I was finally big enough so they couldn't hit me.

Until I wasn't.

Pretty soon, it was someone else's turn, because once you prove that one wrong, there's always another one waiting in the wings—to clip your wings. There was always someone to take Sam's place, or Lyndsay's, or _____ (fill in the blank). **NAME**

After thirteen years in LA, I didn't just get hit—I was pummeled.

If we can't become big enough, does that mean we aren't enough?

I spent my entire life allowing the hurt, the rejection, the utter cruelty to fuel me, but I had nothing left. Literally, I had done everything I possibly could; there was no more fueling, no more running. I had no choice but to sit in it.

To sit with her.

225

kiersten lyons

I was suddenly right back at that seventh-grade dance, my heart racing at Sam G.'s words, so confused because I'd been so sure this time would be different. Thirty minutes before the dance I had shown up to Lauren's house in my usual ensemble—the back of the Land's End catalogue seasonal clearance section (because my mom refused to buy fad clothing that would just go out of style). With one look, Lauren and her mom whisked me away.

Because let's not forget the tennis racket earring in JUST ONE EAR!

I entered Martin Luther King Jr. Middle School's dance with curled hair, a turquoise t-shirt with sleeves that rolled up to purple, and Lauren's denim overalls with one strap undone. I had done everything I should have.

And still Sam G. called me an alien.

I loved James with everything I had.

crushed

And still he didn't want me.
I poured everything into my dreams.
And still Hollywood closed every door.
If we can't prove them wrong, does that mean they're right?
Are we the sum of what people say about us? Am I ugly? A reject? A loser?

Because by Taylor's speech, the speech I dreamed of one day making, the speech that was the theme of my entire life: I am all those things and more. I wasn't suddenly at that seventh-grade dance: I had been there all along.

Because spending our lives constantly proving the negativity wrong doesn't fuel us—it controls us.

If we truly want to have peace, we have to do the very thing that we're told not to: We have to honor the pain.

We have to get crushed.

Only then can we truly have hope, because we can finally heal. If we don't, we will just be running the rest of our lives.

It all started when my Spotify apparently judged me for listening to the *Waitress* Broadway soundtrack for the 107th time because in the middle of me belting out "You Matter to Me," it started playing random songs in the same theme: Taylor, Maren, Olivia, Selena, and then suddenly the strikingly familiar piano keys of a song I hadn't heard in decades.

My body registered it, tears immediately forming as I realized the notes were to "It's You I Like" by Mister Rogers.

kiersten lyons

But it wasn't Fred's kind voice; it was a girl's: gentle and slow, but ever so clear. I quickly swiped my car's screen to see an artist named Ellie Schmidly. Her album cover was her as a little girl with a bowl cut and wide smile. Our similarities weren't lost on me, but I had no time to take it in as I needed to swipe back to my onscreen map to get where I was going.

I weaved in and out of traffic, finding myself singing along to a song I was sure I had forgotten. Hearing Ellie's cover, I was struck with the notion that a song once created as a reminder for children to know how wonderful they are was really for anyone. Anyone who's struggling to love themself. Anyone who needs the reminder they matter. Anyone like…

Me.

"But Kiersten," you might say. "Didn't you already do that way back yonder? Remember when you stopped twisting yourself up like a pretzel to get a guy to like you? You wrote a whole award-winning one-woman show about it."

I did, and thank you for acknowledging it was award winning—not many do—but here's the thing about healing: Healing, like grief, isn't linear; it is layered. Healing doesn't follow a timeline or a playbook, and sometimes it shows up at the most inopportune moments.

Like when you're stuck in heavy Atlanta traffic, and you're so overwhelmed by a song from your childhood that you miss a critical exit because you're still getting used to this new town that you never would've moved to in the first place but you and Bradley lost so much work because of the pandemic and abruptly had to break your lease in Brooklyn. Which was devastating for so many reasons, not least of which that you had decided you were ready

crushed

to go back into the entertainment business and were just starting to reach out to people again, you know, like that manager from years before who now said she just wasn't "holy shit excited about you," and why does it feel like you're constantly getting whacked in the face with life and you're always just a loser?! (And if this is all confusing then you skipped the author's note. AND WHY WOULD YOU DO THAT?)

So, yeah. Very layered.

I eventually figured out how to get home, forgetting about the song, but Spotify didn't, because just a few days later while I was trying to drink my coffee in peace like any normal human would, those familiar notes began to play once more.

One might say it was rude. One could also say it was necessary, and not just for me, but for my daughters, too. Because as much as I tried to instill in Ashley and our youngest daughter that they don't need to do anything to prove their worth, Ellie Schmidly's cover made me realize that these two precious girls were still watching as their mom ran around trying to prove her own.

Another layer was exposed, and it was raw, but it was also different this time...because I was different. It was time to do the scary thing: time to stop running because it was only ever in circles, in a cage I had allowed others to create around me. *I* created around me. I wanted to be free of the need to prove others wrong. To prove my worth. To prove I mattered.

Because it is one layer of healing to stand on a stage and tell your childhood stories for a show, but it is a whole other layer to sit with your childhood self and really look at her. To see her. To know her.

To tell her, "It's You I Like."

And look, I didn't set out to sing to photos of my little girl self, but just like the woman at the church so many years before, this song just showed up in my life and offered a peace I couldn't resist.

I pulled the first photo out, feeling somewhat silly singing to tiny me. She had yet to have been called a loser, have an action figure thrown at her, yet to be told she was ugly or gross, yet to be rejected.

crushed

But then I flipped to this one.

I was ashamed of how much I wanted to *not* look, because all I saw was a girl so desperate to be loved. Ashamed of her loud voice and gangly body and then ashamed of feeling this about myself. Ashamed of my fragmented life filled with confidence and self-hatred. Ashamed of how years before, a boy I liked saw this picture and threw it across the room, laughing and yelling, "Goooooo!" Ashamed because I laughed too, so disassociated from the pain, from her. But now I just stared at a little girl I wanted so badly to protect. A little girl who so deeply just wanted someone to see her, all of her: with her growing-out bowl cut, her flat chest, her loud mouth, her chicken legs, she needed someone to say, "I'm sorry you feel so alone. I'm sorry you feel ugly. These are big

kiersten lyons

feelings, and they hurt so much, but they aren't true. They are a lie. You don't need to grow up to be worthy. You don't need to be famous to be seen. You don't need to be chosen by someone you see as better to finally matter."

Because it's you I love.

I looked at her once more, tears pouring down my cheeks, then I closed my eyes, shut them tight, and walked into that seventh-grade dance.

My eyes scanned the room, the DJ's head bopped to Boys II Men, kids crowded around a table lined with Doritos bags and Capri-Suns, and a little girl with one denim overall strap undone walked by.

I was such a little girl.

I saw little me get asked to slow dance, her face beaming as she swayed back and forth just like she'd seen Cory and Topanga do it in *Boy Meets World*. The song ended and the boy walked her over to the table with the Capri-Suns. I saw myself reach for a Pacific Cooler as Sam walked over, his face twisted in a smile. I watched her as Sam said those cruel words, tears welling up, but she blinked hard, keeping them down.

Except this time, I didn't.

I cried the tears I didn't allow myself to cry that night. I cried for the years that I never felt heard, never felt I mattered. I cried that I had allowed this knot to be so deeply woven into me, that I allowed people to treat me the way they did. Over and over.

Then I held her little face in my hands and told her the truth as the song washed over us both.

crushed

"I'm sorry you feel so alone. I'm sorry you feel ugly. These are big feelings, and they hurt so much but they aren't true. They are a lie. You don't need to grow up to be worthy. You don't need to be famous to be seen. You don't need to be chosen by someone you see as better to finally matter. *Because it's you I love.*"

And then I turned to Sam.

Sam was short, shorter than all the other boys, and he knew it. We all knew it, but somehow as he called me an alien, I was frozen. Knowing it wasn't okay to call out a boy's height, even as he called out everything about me.

His scowl was still pointed in my direction, making sure the guy I had just slow danced with knew what a grave mistake he made. Because I was a grave mistake.

He was laughing now, his "pleased with himself" face looked like my big brother's, like so many who would say such mean things.

How could they be so heartless? How could anyone be so cruel? How could—

Shhh. Be cool! Lyndsay is walking towards us. Oh, wait… no. He's just walking towards the Capri-Suns.

Oh shit… Lyndsay…

No longer was Boys II Men belting out a slow song; now it was just the familiar sound of an old school bus chugging up a hill as Lyndsay asked me about chapstick.

Crap!

I saw little me sitting there looking from Lyndsay to Nate and back to Lyndsay. I watched her trying to figure out what to do as Lyndsay went on and on about chapstick until she finally….

kiersten lyons

"I know, I can't believe how poor some people are that they can't afford chapstick."

Nate's face immediately turned, trying to hide the tears that were already forming. *The tears I helped cause.*

Why couldn't I just have stopped Lyndsay, told him to shut up? I had stuck up for other kids on that same bus before; why was I so quick to be cruel this time? So quick to cause harm?

I looked at my little face, oblivious to the pain I just caused because how could anyone see anything other than the fact that Lyndsay was looking at me? He was finally seeing how wrong he was! In that moment, I had the evidence I had so desperately craved: I was likeable…lovable, even. I was worthy. Because if someone like Lyndsay said I mattered, I must, right?

Except we all know Lyndsay got off the bus. We all know that I would spend the rest of my life trying to get him and others like him back on.

Guys, if you could just see, if you could just… then I would….

I watched little me looking at Nate, taking in all that she had just done. What would that moment have been if I had believed Mister Rogers's words? If I already knew I mattered and had nothing to prove?

What if I had believed in my own dignity? Would I then been able to see Nate's?

What would countless moments in our lives be if we knew our value, our worth?

For the first time, maybe ever, I sat with the understanding of how lost I really was. How anyone is when they can hurt like I did. Because I wasn't acting from a place of worth

crushed

or dignity, I was acting from a place of longing, of loneliness, of desperately trying to belong.

Trying to prove is just trying to belong. Trying to decide who we are by others' opinions. Others who also were hurtful...lost.

I have spent my entire life allowing people who don't know who they are tell me who I am.

I'd actually had this thought a few years before, right after an Al-Anon meeting (remember when I said healing isn't linear), but it hit so different as I sat on the bus with Nate. And for the first time I was grateful, like really and truly grateful that Lyndsay had gotten off the bus.

If he stayed, I might've rested my whole worth in that moment, in that proof. If I'd gotten that approval, fulfilled my dreams, been famous, it would've all settled in me from a place of power over others to feel enough instead of the innate knowledge that I was always enough to begin with. My whole self would've been centered on another's opinion of me, on accolades, on the rushing tide of their acceptance, instead of the truth.

I might've been able to say, "Look at me now!" but I actually wouldn't have ever been able to look at myself.

I sit in this humility often, in the realization that I am human, and that everyone else is too. I don't mean I still allow others to hurt me over and over, but when others are human, I see that they are doing the best they can with what they have, and often what they are doing doesn't have much to do with me anyway.

It actually says a whole lot more about them.

kiersten lyons

And so, I take a breath, remind myself what's true, and oftentimes schedule another therapy appointment, because —let's say it all together—healing isn't linear. And that's perhaps the most hopeful thing of all, because the more we learn about ourselves, the more we can love—others, and most *especially* ourselves.

This is what leads to hope, what leads to peace, what leads to freedom.

When my therapist wasn't yammering on about how the only that's constant in life is change, she was offering a meditation that I mostly didn't want because it would force me to do all this: to look at myself, to change things up, to admit maybe I didn't always know what's best, you know…to let go.

Please note: What I did to Nate (and Ivan) came from a place of hurt, yes, but that doesn't mean it was okay that I allowed that hurt to then hurt them. I wish I could take it all back, but I can't, I can only take responsibility.

N and I, I am truly sorry I allowed my own wounds to bleed onto you. I am sorry in my quest for worth, I tore into yours. It wasn't fair or deserved, it was just mean.

But I've been whacked upside the head enough times in life to know when my ways aren't working, that probably means it's time to try something new. And so, begrudgingly I said out loud, "God give me the grace to see what You want me to see."

And I had no idea what I was in for.

Chapter Twenty-Four

hope

It was his birthday, and I couldn't think of anything sweeter than making him a little video telling him how much he meant to me.

Oh no, not Bradley...Jonathan Taylor Thomas.

I was in overall shorts (both straps clicked this time) with my phone suctioned to the window for the best possible light.

Look, I'm learning to fall in love with myself, sure, but you bet I will still always search out the best lighting.

I held the soft pouch envelope that contained the dozens of letters I had written over the years to my future husband. Letters from when I was so sure he was somebody he most definitely wasn't. Letters from college, from high school, from that fourteen-year-old girl. I pulled out the one that I'd chosen to be displayed in lobby for every single *Crushed* performance, the one I have read aloud on stage and countless times in my apartment, the one that is so hilarious now but was so heartbreaking then.

The letter I started this book with.

kiersten lyons

It's on recycled wide-ruled paper (a staple of the '90s). In my quest to take care of the environment, I hadn't thought what time would do to the already thin paper. I gently unfolded it, careful to respect the history of it all, as I began to read it out loud for the camera, for Jonathan.

"February 2, 199—"

I suddenly stopped, my eyes staring at the date. How had I never noticed this before?! I grabbed my phone from the mount and called Ashley.

"When were you born? What's your birthdate?!"

"Kiki, you know my birth—"

"I know. I just need you to say it!"

"Okay…February 2, 1996."

The day I wrote this letter, the day I was searching for hope, was the day Ashley was born. The literal day she came to be.

I wouldn't meet her for another nine and half years, and she wouldn't move in and begin calling us her other parents for another eight and half after that, but I'm completely struck with the plot twist of a fourteen-year-old girl crying about boys at the same moment her future daughter is crying her first breaths of life.

I had no idea that one of the greatest loves of my life was out there. I had no idea how much I could love another. I was and am surprised by the gift of saying yes. It wasn't someone finally saying "Yes," to me; it was me saying "Yes," to another.

How many other surprises were waiting for me, just across the tears, the heartbreak, the crushing blows?

How many surprises are waiting for you?

crushed

Just before we knew Ashley was moving in, we bought tickets to Hawaii (well, our Delta SkyMiles bought them, but you get what I'm saying). Bradley, our then one-year-old daughter and I were heading to Oahu where Bradley's brother was stationed. His brother was about to deploy, and so his whole family was descending on their house—literally. We were all staying there (it was the only way Bradley and I could afford the trip).

But now that Ashley was moving in, I felt sick at the thought of leaving her back home. She was part of our family now, but with the move, deposit, and higher rent, we had literally no money. A friend suggested a GoFundMe, but I felt embarrassed at the thought of telling everyone we couldn't afford her plane ticket. But I got over that real quick, because that's the thing about constantly getting humbled, constantly getting crushed: you realize doing the solid thing is way better than looking solid.

So, we set up a link, and within two hours of sharing it, her ticket (and then some) was paid for. I was astounded at the generosity of our family and friends in such a short time. But even more astounding? Even more surprising? The first person who donated.

Brian.

The boy twenty-two-year-old me had been so sure was my person was now making sure Ashley could go.

I used to think I was doing healing all wrong, because how could I still be so hurt? But then I wrote it down, the hard, the bad, the hilarious, and I began to see the truth: There is always goodness to be found, and it doesn't mean

kiersten lyons

it still won't hurt, or we still won't have days where we can barely get out of bed; it means we are always one moment away from asking for the grace to see what we need to see.

Therapy, support groups, medicine, and journaling were all tools that helped me to get here, but more importantly: to stay here.

Chapter Twenty-Five

dear you (again)

Remember all the way back on page 73 I asked you to write down three things to eventually play a game? Well, it's time!

But before we get into it, I want you to find a picture of little you. It can be on your phone or one that's framed in your childhood home, but one where you can clearly see you, because it's time to clearly *see*.

(And if for some reason life hasn't allowed you childhood mementos, if you're struggling to find a picture of little you, then take a breath, because that's not fair. And when you're ready, and if it feels safe, close your eyes and find a moment when you were little, when your shoes were tiny, and your dreams were big. Because even if there isn't a physical picture to look at, little you still deserve to be seen.)

Next, head over to that *Crushed* playlist to find Ellie Schmidly's cover of "It's You I Like."

Okay, let's play some Mad Libs.

kiersten lyons

My name is _____.
NOUN
I was born on _____ in _____ . It
BIRTHDAY   PLACE
was a beautiful day no matter if it was raining or sunny, no matter
if I came into the world expected and planned or a complete
surprise. It was beautiful because every little baby is beautiful.
Every little soul is enough.

I am _____ years old in this picture, and my
AGE
favorite color was _____. This was important because
COLOR
it was important to her.

Because she is important.

It doesn't mean people haven't told her different, maybe even
over and over, it just means they aren't telling the truth. They don't
actually know her, because they don't know themselves, and if they
did, they wouldn't have ever said those things to her.

Her favorite stuffy was _____ . Holding it close
NAME
made her feel _____ because she loved it so much. It
EMOTION
doesn't look new anymore; it may have gotten dropped or dragged,
washed or forgotten, but it is still so beautiful, so treasured, so
valuable.

She looks different now too. She may have even gotten
dropped, dragged through the mud, or even forgotten, but that
doesn't make her any less valuable, any less treasured, any less
beautiful.

She was enough. I am enough.

crushed

Someday her favorite color might change, and what once was so significant may not feel so needed anymore. That's okay. She can change. She can let go of things that used to feel so important, but that doesn't mean she's any less important.

Because no matter what, she matters. Every part of her. Her skin, her eyes, her feelings, whether old or new. Because it's her I like.

It's her I love.

Epilogue

"What state are you in?"

Our social worker's voice was quick, as I tried to remember exactly where we were. In the last two months we'd been in twice as many states. New York, Delaware, Tennessee, and now Virginia.

"You must stay there. You can't go anywhere else."

"But you said we could move to Atlanta? The judge said—"

It was May of 2020.

"The court changed their minds—you have to be in a state our agency is licensed in, even with the pandemic."

"For how long?"

"Until the adoption is finalized, and with the courts backed up because of everything, we don't know when that will be...but if you move, you risk losing your son."

We risk losing our son.

Oh, yeah—also we have a son!

It all happened so fast: we got the call March 1, 2020: a mom had chosen our family to place her newborn; the next day we met him and her; by March 8, we were back in Brooklyn, and on March 14, listening to the advice of our

crushed

pediatrician and social workers, we left our seven-hundred-square-foot apartment to stay with family until this whole thing "blew over." First in Tennessee with Bradley's parents and then to Virginia with my Aunt Ginny.

But we all know it didn't exactly blow over; like so many, our whole world was cracked open; we'd lost too much work to afford Brooklyn any longer and had to break our lease and our dreams of watching our kids grow up in our favorite city. And because our new adoption agency was only licensed in six states, our choices for immediate housing were small.

I say new adoption agency because right at the last moment, after background checks and trainings, interviews, and a full home study, we began to see red flags at the adoption agency we thought we had vetted so carefully.

The cult had taught me to follow the money; James had taught me to trust my gut; Ashley had taught me it's not my narrative; and now all were pointing to us leaving.

Adoption can be incredibly unethical, filled with coercion and even straight up lies, so equipped with my therapist's stupid meditation that kept bringing us towards peace (but away from the easy thing that I swear would just be so great!), Bradley and I went back to the drawing board.

And after over a year into the process, we switched to a much smaller adoption agency, only licensed in six states (as opposed to all fifty as our original one) but with much more support for both adoptees and birth parents. Our new agency's approach to centering the adoptee and birth family as well as understanding the trauma and loss of adoption was everything we could hope for. It also would mean us losing

kiersten lyons

out on money we didn't have, but we knew if we stayed with the old one, we'd never have the peace we had learned time and time again was far greater than the comfortable.

But now looking at my phone as my social worker explained next steps, I realized we were once again smack dab in the middle of choosing love, of choosing humans over bricks, and I would be lying if I said I wasn't scared of the unknown.

But there was no need. Aunt Ginny, who we call our Fairy Godmother (she's only my godmother Bradley—step off!), invited our little family in with open arms without knowing for how long. She took in a first grader doing Zoom school, a newborn baby, and two exhausted parents trying to cobble together work from her kitchen table all while she still had to work from her dining table. It was the sweetest gift and one I realize comes with immense privilege at having such incredible support systems in the unmerited grace of such deep care.

Aunt Ginny was with us every step of the way, honoring our little guy's first mama, celebrating birthdays and anniversaries and just making the most challenging days truly extraordinary. We lived so much life around that little kitchen table, including having to update our home study with her home. When our social worker asked her over Zoom how she felt about all of us in her home, she took a breath and looked into camera:

"I won't lie, it is hard sometimes and loud often, but it's also beautiful. It's not just me giving them a place to stay; they are giving me family. My daughter is across the country,

crushed

I'm still working from home, and if they didn't need me, I would've been by myself this entire time."

Bradley and I would have never chosen to lose work, to lose our apartment, but I also never would want to give up those nine months at Aunt Ginny's. I would never give up any of the goodness, the surprises, the immense healing of getting *Crushed* over and over. Because life is full of *Crushed* moments; sometimes we are the ones offering a home, and sometimes we are the ones needing one.

The same is true for you.

There will be a day your heartbreak won't feel so close, where you won't need this book anymore, and you'll pass it off (just kidding, publisher—they won't let a friend borrow it; they'll definitely purchase a new book). There will be a day when you won't need my story anymore because you'll be writing your own.

In fact, you already are.

Acknowledgments

Here's the thing: I honestly didn't think I'd ever get to this page because (and congrats, Cheryl, you're finally up to speed on this) NOTHING IN MY LIFE GOES THE WAY I PLAN. This book was no exception, with lots of pivots all the way, but you are holding it, and I couldn't be more grateful I get to give all the people below their flowers.

Bradley, there is no way any of this would've happened without you. "For serious," as little E would say. Your constant belief in me and unwavering support is the reason I have said from the beginning, "I can't believe you exist." (Okay, not at the beginning, because as we all know I was an idiot and ghosted you, but you get what I mean.) Thank you for listening as I read you page after page after another page only to change it again after I swore *that was the last edit!* Your absolute care in making space and sitting beside me as I went back into old emails and old feelings was nothing short of holy. Thank you for listening to me as I processed stuff I had no idea I still needed to process and making me laugh throughout the entire thing. You are our steady calm in the storm while simultaneously making the boat rock with laughter, and all of this is the reason I will forever call you

crushed

Bradley Best (also you cook every meal, every day). And if that was it, it would still be too much, but then you take me to Disney (when it's the last place you want to be) and buy my Mickey ice cream bars. What I'm saying is I'm taken with you too.

Ashley, I kinda wish I was saying this to you instead of writing it in a book because one of my favorite things is showering you with compliments and watching you squirm. I cannot believe when this book comes out, we will have known each other for twenty years. You are, without a doubt, the most loyal, loving, and compassionate young woman I've ever known. Dadley and I are beyond honored we have gotten a front row seat to your growing up, and I couldn't begin to express how grateful I am that Sandra matched us. My sweet girl, thank you for allowing me the gift of being your Big Sister turned other Mom—I will never get over the gift of who you are.

E and L, you are both woven throughout this entire book, even though almost all of it takes place before each of you were even born. Getting to be your mama is the best present I get to unwrap daily (even when I quote *Bluey* and "just need twenty minutes"). There is no way this book would be here without our family dance parties, Saturday morning breakfasts, and so many mama cuddles.

Jen, your care for not only *Crushed* but also me is unmatched. I have NEVER had a rep who was so kind, yet so good at what she does. I will never forget the day I got your email that said, "I really want you to know that I think you

kiersten lyons

have something magical here." It is you who are magical and just thank you from the bottom of my heart for everything.

Kate, I know you already know I googled you before we met, and I can't begin to share the excitement (and nerves) I had before our first call because I was so sure you were the editor for this project. I am so glad for once in my life I was right! I am beyond grateful for your hard work, honesty, and above all, love of this book. I couldn't have asked for a better editor. Maddie, your attention to detail (and attention to all my many emails that swore "it was just one more thing") is so beyond appreciated. Jim, the cover design is everything! Your openness to collaboration mixed with your talents was something other authors can only hope for (truly, so many of my writer friends are so jealous when I tell them how amazing it all was). Alana, the interior of the book feels like something I ripped out of my eighth-grade notebook and my dreams. Thank you for the thoughtfulness that covers each page and each hand-drawn doodle. Gretchen, without you I would still be swimming in a sea of publishers who "didn't know what to do with it." Thank you for passing it to Kate, thank you for believing in it from the very beginning. To everyone at Regalo Press who read, edited, and championed this book, thank you from the bottom of my no longer broken heart.

To my parents: you taught me to not only laugh at the hard stuff but also dig deeper and ask the big questions. Thank you for showing up always, whether it was tons of school plays, swim meets, or flying across the country to visit your struggling actress daughter. Okay, well, not always, you know I can't miss a chance to revisit the tee ball game you

crushed

missed where I made a home run. *AND YES LUKE, tee ball home runs are still legit home runs!* Mom and Dad, thank you for giving me the gumption to go for it and the safe place to land when the "it" didn't turn out the way I wanted. I love you both.

Luke, Jack, Hallie, and Annie, from our shared bowl cuts (well, except for Jack because apparently he was "too cute" for the Lyons tradition) to sharing DNA, thank you for letting me share so much of our childhood here. Getting to watch each of you grow up into amazing parents and people (who occasionally laugh at my jokes) is such a honor and I love the five of us so much (but also am really glad we can all have our own box of fries now). *Crushed* would not be what it is without each of you, but neither would I.

Aunt Ginny, *Crushed* wouldn't be here without your out-of-this-world gift of a home for nine months but equally your gift of Disney World. Both gave me breath to remember it's okay to not have everything figured out and okay to be child-like. Thank you for always asking "how are you?" but also allowing me to ask you the same. I am beyond grateful my mom prayed so hard for a baby sister.

Erin, YOU are the reason this book is even kind of a thing. Your constant efforts in sending me TikTok after TikTok inflating my ego by just simply texting, "you could do this so much better," was a masterclass in manipulation. Plus, co-hosting *Crushed the Podcast* was one of the greatest joys of my life. You are the greatest cousin of all time, such a safe space for E, and yes, I purposely put your thank-you just above Chris's.

kiersten lyons

Chris, I can't thank you enough for the care you took in writing the forward and even more so for being such an integral part of my growing up. Watching you become an incredible husband and father is truly one of my favorite things I've ever gotten to see, only matched by seeing your videos with Erin (your wife, not my cousin) that remind me so much of your humble beginnings in gumballs (I'm really hoping I'm getting the name right) on a VHS. Thank you for being my LA big brother.

Julie and Kristina—I'm not sure if you both understand how integral you were in getting this book out there. Both of you have cheered my words from the beginning and so loudly. Kristina, you sharing your own book proposal with me opened this whole thing up, and Julie, you being the first to read this book in its entirety gave me the confidence to keep going. I cannot even begin to explain what each of your encouragement meant to me throughout this whole process.

Emmy and fam—being with you all as my life untangled and then was brought back together was such a gift. And getting to have Teddy sit on my lap through it all I will forever cherish. Thank you for being my family when my own was across the country.

Natalie, it's not even kind of dramatic to say you are such a large part of this book, both in creation and care. Your love for both L and E allowed me the time and space to write so much, but it was your creativity that helped me knit together so many bits and pieces of this whole book. From cover ideas to being the first person who read the sample chapters,

crushed

your fingerprints are all over this book and I couldn't be more grateful!

Tina, Amy, Steve, Carol, Martin, Mindy, and Maya—this isn't how I planned to tell you how much your wit, humor, and authenticity have shaped me. I really thought we'd bump into each other at an awards show or red carpet or, at least, a dinner party at Lorne's house. Either way, even though we've never met, each of you have taught me how to spin words to spin heads and to forever be fully myself. Thank you.

To everyone who didn't love me back, thank you. Your rejection created content, but even more it helped me find who I was created to be.

Cori, I'm not sure a day went by where I didn't wish I could read you a line or a page or the whole damn thing. There were so many times after writing I would close my eyes and think of your contagious laughter listening as I read it out loud. I don't think it's a coincidence that this book first went out to publishers on St. Francis of Assisi's feast day, the guy whose prayer we read as we said goodbye to you, and the guy who I refer to often when I miss you. And I do miss you. So much.

This book is because of you.

About the Author

Kiersten Lyons is an actress, writer, and lactose intolerant. Her most notable roles include being attacked by her pet lion on *Grey's Anatomy*, being accused of murdering the husband she shared with her sister wives on *Bones*, and the real-life role of having her wedding called off two months shy of the date, which resulted in the award-winning one-woman show, *Crushed: Why Is It That the Boys You Like, Never Like You Back?*

For the better part of her whole life, she's been a big sister, by biology, through Big Brothers Big Sisters, and now on social media, sharing real stories and hilarious observations that have amassed tens of millions of views. Her unique voice has created a tight-knit community of young women eager to laugh, cry, and heal. You can find her at kierstenlyons.com.

And, yes, she was the girl who once made Taylor Swift cry happy tears…